Diaspora Journey:
A Passover Haggadah Drama
REVISED EDITION

by
Corey-Jan Albert

ISBN 978-0-557-32223-7

Table of Contents

iii

Acknowledgments

Diaspora Journey: A Passover Haggadah Drama began as my Master's Thesis at Georgia State University. As it has progressed, many people have supported me with their knowledge, love and support.

I don't think anyone could have as wonderful a collection of friends as I do. Dr. Martha Rosenthal has been there to talk about liminality and Haggadot since we planned our first Seder together in 1992. I probably would never have embarked on this project without her. Deb Calabria, my erstwhile partner in graduate study crimes, shared her keen directorial eye with me and helped me find the right ending for the egg story. My cousin, Nancy Schwartz Katz, an exceptional artist, well known for her gorgeous Jewish and secular work, created the cover image portraying the scene in which Moses simultaneously breaks the matzoh in two and parts the sea. Andrea Abelman has been a wonderful friend to me, even changing plans to go out of town so she and her family could attend my Seder each year. She makes a mean Matzoh ball, too. Kimberly Reingold has been my partner in Hebrew studies, creative idea generation, problem solving and running - and I am ever grateful for her friendship and encouragement. Rabbi Pamela Gottfried, who shares my passion for Passover and Haggadot, spurred me to create this revised edition, which now closely matches the order of traditional Passover Seders. My work and I are better for her knowledge, her input, her friendship and her way with DavkaWriter. Rabbi Brad Levenberg reviewed this several times and continues to impress me with his intelligence and humor. All of my friends get major points for putting up with me during the times when I've focused on little but this project.

Even though it has been a long time since I completed my Master's degree, this project would not exist without the extraordinary thesis committee members who advised me through its initial inception. I first began thinking about writing a Haggadah when one of Rabbi Phil Kranz's 1990 or 1991 High Holy Day sermons encouraged congregation members to engage themselves "more creatively" with Jewish tradition and liturgy. Whether or not this is what he had in mind, Rabbi Kranz somehow managed to find time amidst his schedule as spiritual leader of Temple Sinai in Atlanta and professor at several universities to read iterations of this project, to discuss ideas and theology with me, to help me create language where none existed and to share both his books and his valuable insights. Dr. Marian Meyers had never worked with me on anything prior to this project, yet she was always thorough in her readings, deep in her insights and quick with both criticism and praise. She never seemed too busy to talk with me or come to a meeting and I believe my work is stronger for her input. Dr. Ray Miller was extremely generous with his knowledge of anthropology, ritual and performance, as well as his natural curiosity, warmth and understanding. He never ceases to surprise me with the depth and breadth of his library and knowledge and I consider myself fortunate to have worked with him. Last, but certainly not least, the unsinkable Dr. Gayle Austin gave me her enthusiasm and support for this project, tireless readings, a willingness to meet with me during odd hours, and some outstanding dramaturgical suggestions. She served as my primary teacher and advisor throughout my studies at Georgia State and I am most grateful for her time, attention and encouragement.

Lucky me, my mother is and has always been my friend. Even though this is not the kind of thing that Joice Albert ever would write, she was always there to read it and discuss it with me. She has shared her love and her personal understanding of both the Holocaust and Russian Pogroms with me. I am especially appreciative of how thoroughly and enthusiastically she has supported my work as a writer.

My mother-in-law, Sara Deitch, gave me a great deal of her time, reading several iterations of this piece and offering thoroughly detailed suggestions for improvement. I should also mention how grateful I am for the times when, as the Temple Sinai librarian, she generously pointed me toward relevant source material and willingly ignored due dates for books.

My father-in-law, Milton Deitch, has always tried to maintain a sense of tradition and decorum at all the Seders at his house. So I wondered how he might respond to such a non-traditional Haggadah as this. To my delight, he has been willing to participate in the development of this project, even if he has seemed a bit bemused by how "different" it is.

To explain my father, Sam Albert's, contribution to this project, I must recount a bit of family history. At the end of all our family Seders, Dad would sing Chad Gadya. Upon getting to "Rezabenabbabisrezuzah..." (which he sang as if it were all one word), he would bang his fist on the table and shout, "Hey!" before singing the end. All of us learned to follow the unwritten stage direction to lift our wine glasses at this point because if we didn't, the impact of my dad's voice and fist would send wine flying, invariably into the lap of the only person wearing white (me, on two occasions). So my father gets the credit for first pointing out how theatrical Seders can be. He played Moses in every Seder at my house until his untimely death in 2003. It would be impossible for me to think of Passover and not think of him; I dedicate this text to his memory.

During the years when I worked on this project, we were very fortunate to have included nine amazing young women in our family as au pairs. Their experiences and perspectives have given me so much to think about and enjoy. Güneş Erdoḡan of Turkey helped me get through my comprehensive exams. Una Eydís Finnsdóttir of Iceland helped me get through the research and writing of the prospectus for this project. Petra Huck of Germany (and New Zealand) helped me through the final writing and defense of *Diaspora Journey*. Veronique Gerbit of France, Kersin Mueller of Germany, Liene Berzina of Latvia, Kristin Solvang of Norway, Ania Bosowiec (now Alford) of Poland (and now the U.S.), and Christiane Kleine-Koenig of Germany all participated in Seders using this text and engaged in many a meaningful discussion about religion, politics, history and family. So, to all of them, I say saul, tak, danke, merci, danke, pateiciba, tak, dziekuja and danke. And remember what I told you: once you become family, you can never be un-family again.

Many of these people, as well as several other friends and family members – Lyn and Den Baldauf, Debbie and Frank Butterfield, Pam Willoughby and Paul Chen, Lisa and Paul Marquardt, Theresa Cohen, David Deitch, Jonathan Deitch, Anna Deitch, Audrey Galex, Joe and Jeanette Leader, and Jessica Wood – participated in the first Seder/ reading of this Haggadah. I offer my deepest gratitude for their creativity, their willingness to try something completely different, their friendship and their love. I also wish to thank Elaine Blumenthal, Rae Goodman, Jennifer Cohen, Minda Gordon and the women of the Ahavath Achim Rosh Hodesh women's group for their support, their enthusiasm, and for pointing out how well the music of Debbie Friedman would fit with my text. And I thank the people at SoundsWrite productions for letting me include it.

My multi-talented children, Cameron and Maxxe, have grown up with this Haggadah, breathing life into the text, playing a variety of roles with equal parts talent and passion. My work is so much stronger for all the two of them bring to it.

Finally, the most thanks must go to my husband, Joel Deitch, for his love, support, editing and willingness to discuss this project with me at all hours of the day and night. Joel's historical knowledge and love of learning have always impressed me – and I took every advantage of those qualities while working on this project. I must admit to waking Joel from restful sleep at 3:00 AM to discuss some plot turn or Judaic issue on more than one occasion - and he was always willing (if not quite awake) to engage in those discussions. He is a terrific husband, partner, parent, friend and I love him.

Introduction

A Starting Point for Change

The Jewish Passover Seder is a ritual dinner commemorating the biblical Exodus. It involves all dinner participants in a re-telling of the story by way of a text called a Haggadah (literally, "The Telling," translated from Hebrew). The experience of participating in a Seder is meant to be powerful, rejuvenating and even magical; recollections of our ancestors echo anew, year after year, reflected in the ever changing reality of our present times.[1] At least, that is how the experience is supposed to feel. Unfortunately, the Seder experience for many Jews, particularly Reform and Conservative Jews in America, has become less vibrantly connective.

Growing up in New York as the daughter of a father raised in a rigid, Orthodox household and a mother comfortably secular in her approach to spiritual matters, the Seders I remember were more about family togetherness than spiritual engagement. In fact, we always practiced the "Readers Digest" version of the Haggadah, skipping quickly through the text to specific highlights. And forget about the four questions – the only real question on anybody's mind was, "When do we eat?!" As I began exploring my own spirituality, I found that, to varying degrees, many family Seders in America had similar dynamics. The more deeply I explored the evolution of Haggadot, the more I was bothered by the androcentricity of the text and ritual, as well as the paradox of an inherently dramatic ritual whose performative potential is never fully realized.

A Tradition of Evolving Perspectives

Throughout history, there have been hundreds of thousands of published Haggadot.[2] The oldest Haggadah in existence today dates back to 13th century Spain and is filled with brightly colored pictures which direct participants exactly how to perform the rituals of the Seder.[3] In the 14th century, Haggadot evolved to place more emphasis on the story of the Exodus. The first *printed* Haggadah was created from woodcuts published in Prague in 1521.[4] Today's Orthodox Haggadah differs little from these original texts and is used in many Seders (both Orthodox and non-Orthodox).

A tradition of transforming the Haggadah text to reflect the world since the time of the Exodus, however, also exists. Arthur Waskow, one of the most renowned "transformers" of the Haggadah notes, "The Haggadah teaches us to rewrite the Haggadah." He adds that especially since the late 1960's, "there has been a growing wave of energy among American Jews, moving toward the renewing and remaking of Jewish thought and practice," particularly the Passover Seder.[5] The Reform, Conservative and Reconstructionist denominations of Judaism each have an "official" Haggadah that differs from the traditional Orthodox text. An increasing number of Feminist Haggadot look at the concepts of the Passover Seder as they pertain to women. The Library of Congress lists hundreds of published Haggadot, each written and/or designed to express a new perspective on the compelling concepts of slavery and liberation. Even more Haggadot are created and used without commercial publication. *Diaspora Journey: A Passover Haggadah Drama,* with its different perceptions of both the content and dramatic structure of the Passover Haggadah, is a natural extension of the longstanding tradition of renewal and reinvention.

The Androcentricity Problem

Traditional Haggadot assume that all participants will be male. They also tend to portray women as insignificant followers whose duties were to serve the men of their tribe and whose primary need was that of male leadership. Women who dared take on a leadership role were severely punished. The primary example of such punishment is noted in the twelfth chapter of Numbers, in which both Moses' sister Miriam and brother Aaron challenge Moses' authority. In response, Miriam is stricken with Leprosy and sent out of the camp for seven days. Aaron receives no such condemnation and is anointed as a priest.[6]

Because the Passover Seder is based in the home, the roles that men and women are directed to play are reflective of a perceived traditional sociology of the home – in which men explain and direct while women cook, serve and support. The heavy male bias of traditional Haggadot may be inaccurate, however – both for the time of the Exodus and the present. Karen Armstrong maintains that during the forty years in which the Jews wandered in the desert, women played a far more important leadership role within the early Jewish community.[7] She further suggests that when the Jews settled in Israel and ceased to be a nomadic culture, these roles were literally rewritten. At the time, monotheistic devotion to the "God of Abraham" had not fully taken root, particularly among the women who maintained varying degrees of loyalty to fertility goddesses. Armstrong cites evidence of a fundamentalist revival during which the men in power probably rewrote the earlier biblical stories to maintain order and keep women in their subservient places within their new social and political hierarchy.[8] Judith Plaskow corroborates the fact that women may have had significantly more power and respect than current liturgy suggests.[9]

Most feminist Haggadot address the obvious gap between the helpless or invisible ways in which women are usually portrayed and the strong capabilities that women have always possessed. I believe that they may do so, however, at the expense of the overall continuum of the Jewish experience, both for men and women.

The Opportunity of Performance

The relationship between ritual and performance has been of great interest to many researchers. Leading work in this area has been done by anthropologist Victor Turner and theatre practitioner/scholar Richard Schechner, both of whose core concepts of liminality in rites of passage stem from the early research of anthropologist Arnold Van Gennep. A vast number of other studies of the relationships between ritual and performance also exist. Most of this research, however, focuses on Asian, African and Native American rituals.

A search of published Haggadot has led me to believe that there are no Haggadot which take direct advantage of the inherent theatricality of the Passover Seder. Elizabeth Swados' musical play, *Haggadah!* addresses many issues in the traditional Passover Seder – in a very compelling way – but this play is meant to be performed in front of an audience, not as an actual Haggadah for a Passover Seder. Several children's Haggadot incorporate puppets, but do not really use drama to highlight the content and rituals of the Seder. Shimon Levy's research into the performative aspects of Haggadot does establish several ways in which the traditional Haggadah is actually a script of a specific performance.[10] Levy stops short, however, of examining ways in which the performative aspects of Haggadot could be enhanced to heighten the communication of the major ideas within the Passover Seder.

The Passover Seder was originally created to encourage involvement and reestablish our connections from past to present and between each other as individuals within the community of Jews.[11] While multiple generations do participate together, the Seder as prescribed in most Haggadot lacks real engagement with the story of the Jews' exodus from Egypt, with the concepts of freedom and slavery, and with the relationship of participants to each other. In most American Seders, the Haggadah is not performed, as much as it is followed. One person (usually male) assumes the authoritarian role of "Leader."[12] He reads most of the Haggadah and everyone else at the table (individually and/or as a group) reads a rote response in turn. The characters are reduced to descriptions of their actions.

Unfortunately, this rote reading means that the messages of the Seder are delivered at the expense of any visceral, emotional connection to the story. Participants who have grown up without knowing the confines of slavery cannot relate emotionally to a command to remember a loss of personal and religious liberty. The Haggadah needs to help bridge the gap and I believe that existing Haggadot do a poor job. Retelling a story by describing it as history and dictating responses to that story still make every event in the story feel like it happened to someone else. Simply adding a few first person lines (e.g. stating that the Seder is performed, "because of what the Lord did for me when I went forth from Egypt,"[13]) is insufficient and hollow.

Bridging the Gaps

I embarked on this project because I felt compelled to reclaim the Haggadah as a performative ritual text, celebrating togetherness within our families and communities at large. Especially in the present-day United States, it seems necessary to reflect a more realistic sociology of the home. Admittedly, most families are far from egalitarian. Women still tend to take on a greater proportion of cooking, cleaning and child rearing tasks than their male partners. Men still make significantly more money than women do. Nevertheless, we lead such busy lives that families have little time to pay homage to pre-established gender roles. Two income families are the norm. Fathers take on a much more active, nurturing role in their children's lives than their own fathers did. It is less and less common to find families in which the father/husband is head of house and the mother/wife is a dependent follower.

It seemed to me that a Haggadah constructed as a play, with interactive characters, could best communicate the inherent emotional power of the Seder. It would engage the audience as entertainment and as a powerful, spiritual ritual. Such a Haggadah could connect past and present and reflect connections between participants as individuals within a family by heightening the liminal experience for all participants. It could acknowledge the roles of women more accurately and involve participants more deeply and tangibly in the performance of Seder rituals. With these ideas in mind, I wrote *Diaspora Journey: A Passover Haggadah/Drama*.

Order and Structure

A Haggadah must include fifteen actions that make up the established structure of the Passover Seder, and note their significance. As long as these fifteen actions (Blessing over the wine, Washing the hands, Dipping greens in salt water, Dividing the middle matzah, Retelling the story of the Jews' bondage in and exodus from Egypt, Washing the hands again, Blessing the bread, Specifically blessing the matzah, Eating bitter herbs, Combining matzah with bitter herbs, Setting the table/Serving the meal, Finding and eating the Afikoman (the concealed middle matzah), Reciting grace, Reciting psalms/Singing songs) are taken, in order, the Seder is legitimately fulfilled.[14] There is no directive indicating that the text be narrative, rather than character-based. My original edition of this Haggadah took some liberties with the traditional order of the Seder. This new revision of *Diaspora Journey* follows the traditional order much more closely as the basis for its structure:

I.   *Illumination/Inspiration*. While the traditional order does not include the lighting of candles, many Jewish rituals do begin with candle lighting.. Aesthetically, the practice of lighting candles is beautiful, spiritual and creative. Theatrically, it commands attention; most dramatic performances begin with lights coming up in a darkened performance space.

II.   *The Four Questions*. Traditionally, the four questions are asked as part of the Magid – the telling of the story of the Jews' slavery in Egypt and subsequent escape. Since the story is revealed throughout the play, however, I thought it appropriate to begin with the traditional questions.

III.   *The First Cup of Wine: Forgetting*. During the seder, participants are to drink four cups of wine. In the context of Diaspora Journey, each of the four cups signifies a mental state change which must take place. The first of these is forgetting – not our past, but our present. Indeed, before we can throw ourselves into our own history, we must forget our present state of being.

IV.   *Water and Greens*. This section combines the first instance of hand washing (U'rhatz) and Greens (Karpas). It also symbolizes what is necessary to grow again when one has lost all that was once familiar.

V.   ***Breaking Apart.*** In this section, the middle matzah (Afikoman) is literally broken apart. In the context of the story, the breaking in half of the Matzah also symbolizes the parting of the Red Sea that facilitated the Jews final escape from the Egyptians. It also illustrates the breaking apart of families that occurs in times of conflict.

VI.   ***Second Cup of Wine: Remembering.*** Once we have forgotten our present state, we are capable of remembering. As this section involves a family of Holocaust victims, this section also echoes the post-Holocaust directive to remember the horrors that almost wiped out the Jews in World War II.

XI.   ***The Ten Plagues/Dayenu/Bread and Sustanance.*** Traditionally, the Passover Seder includes a recitation of the ten plagues that God sent to the Egyptians when Pharaoh would not freely allow the Jews to leave Egypt. Echoed in all of the plagues, however, are ways in which Jews who are not free to practice their religion are afflicted themselves.

Dayenu (דינו) is a Hebrew word meaning, "It would have been sufficient." Typically, the Seder includes a recitation of everything that God did to facilitate the Jews' escape from Egypt and transition to a holy people. After each act of God, participants respond, "Dayenu!" meaning that we are so grateful for every act of God that led to our redemption from slavery that any one of them would have been enough for us. In *Diaspora Journey*, Dayenu is said in response to all the things that Jews have had to give up to survive in hostile surroundings.

Finally, this section contains the washing of hands followed by the blessing for bread and the specific blessing for eating matzah. Just as we attempt to symbolically wash away the plagues that befall us, we are compelled to sustain ourselves, to survive.

VII.   ***Bones.*** Literally, this is a reference to the Shankbone on the table, which references the original Passover sacrifice. Bones are also a metaphor for the old and the dead – the subject of the section.

VIII.   ***Bitterness.*** This refers to the bitter herbs, a symbol of how Pharaoh made the lives of the Jews bitter in Egypt. It also refers to the bitterness of feeling excluded and of fighting amongst ourselves.

IX.   ***Mortar.*** Typically, the Charoset (a mixture of apples, dates, honey and wine) is a symbol of the mortar that the Hebrews used to make bricks in Egypt. It is also a symbol of mortality – the fruit and nuts decay in the fermented wine.[15] Here, I present the Charoset as a symbol of hope, which is the mortar that holds our lives together, even in the most troubling times. As one character says, "We clean up the glass. We rebuild. We move on."

X.   ***Combining.*** In this section, participants combine the bitter herbs with the sweet charoset - the traditional way to eat bitter herbs. The maror and the charoset also are eaten with matzah in a "Hillel Sandwich," commemorating Hillel's tradition of eating bitter herbs together with the paschal lamb. The bitterness of our past and the hope for our future are brought together with a commitment to sustan ourselves. In life, all are necessary to progress.

XIV   ***Roasted Egg. Maternal/Eternal Regenerative Power.*** Although a roasted egg is an essential element of the Seder plate, the presence of the egg is not actually explained in traditional Haggadot. It is often understood to represent offerings brought to the Temple during festivals[16] however there are many other possible explanations for the egg. This section of Diaspora Journey posits several such explanations, including my own, which is that the egg symbolizes the regenerative power of the bonds and relationships between mothers and children.

XI. **_The Meal is Served_**

XII. **_Searching and Finding._** Finding the hidden Afikoman – the middle matzah that is broken during the Seder – and giving it back to the group is necessary to complete the Seder.[19] In _Diaspora Journey,_ however, the Afikoman and the search take on additional meaning. The characters in this drama have all lost something – either a sense of self, a sense of direction, a sense of togetherness or purpose. They must find it before they can move ahead to accept the challenges of the future.

XIII. **_Grace, The Third Cup of Wine and Water in the Desert: Hope_** We give thanks after the meal - and for many things that have become relevant during the Seder thus far. This is immediately followed by the third cup of wine, which in this Seder, signifies hope; once we have forgotten our present, then remembered our past, hope is the only thing that can take us forward into our future. Drinking water is not a traditional element of the Seder as wine is, but I think it should be. Throughout Jewish liturgy, it is maintained that wherever Miriam was in the desert, a well of water followed her, sustaining the Jews.[18] I believe it is important to include water in the Seder, not just as a cleansing element (i.e. used to wash hands), but as a life sustaining one.

XV. **_Wine of Elijah._** The prophet Elijah is supposed to appear as a "protective presence" in times of great vulnerability.[17] It is also said that Elijah will herald the coming of the messiah. We set a place for Elijah, including a glass of wine, to invite this protective, heralding presence into our home. The Seder directs participants to welcome the stranger and/or the "other" into our homes, perhaps because any stranger might indeed be Elijah. There are also other, more practical reasons for opening the door during the Seder, which are addressed in this section. The participants of the Seder literally enter a desert of loneliness, misunderstanding and confrontation. In such a place, even the hope or expectation of a protective presence is most appropriate, even necessary.

XVI. **_More Questions_.** The traditional four questions notwithstanding, I believe that our history compels us to ask other questions, as well. For example, what are we to do with all our history? Why does our history contain so much suffering? If our history and destiny are to be so laden with bitterness, why go on?

XVII. **_The Fourth Cup of Wine: Accepting Challenges._** After reaffirming our hope and finding what we have lost, we are prepared to accept new challenges. As the Seder comes to a close, we emerge renewed and re-centered. We do more than hope for a better future. We consider ways in which we can act upon those hopes.

XVIII **_Singing._** The Passover Seder and Diaspora Journey contain serious, even sorrowful stories. But at heart, this is about survival, our ability to remain together and the perseverence of the human spirit. The Seder must therefore end with all participants singing in celebration together.

I do not include a section about "the four sons" or "the four children" because all the characters in the play can all be characterized as one of the four children (see Casting Options under "Preparation/Direction" below).

Language of God

In writing Diaspora Journey – and indeed, long before I even began work on this project – I struggled mightily with the language we use to refer to God. Traditional Jewish liturgy is extremely limited in its blessing language. God is usually described as some version of, יי אלהינו מלך העולם ("Adonai eloheinu, melech ha'olam," literally, "Lord our God, King (or Ruler) of the universe). As Marcia Falk states, this description of divine power reinforces the concept "of patriarchal power and male privilege in the world."[20] Patriarchy and its associated language are so deeply entrenched in Jewish liturgy that the very act of developing new ways to describe the divine feels risky. As Esther Broner says in her description of what it felt like to create the feminist Haggadah, *The Telling*, "It is still so radical to change the familiar that one's senses are startled."[21]

Finding new language to break away from centuries of androcentricity is daunting. Much contemporary feminist liturgy simply replaces "Adonai eloheinu" with "Shekhinah," a word used in the Zohar, to describe feminine aspects of God. The result is only partially satisfying. According to Gershom Sholem, the Shekhinah is described in the Zohar as "Queen, daughter and bride of God," as "the mother of every individual in Israel" and "the symbol of 'eternal womanhood.'"[22] Describing God only as any of these terms, however, is just as incomplete as describing God only as King, Lord or Father.

Falk, a poet as well as a scholar, imagines new language for the divine. She uses "Eyn hachayim" (source of life), "nitzotzot hanefesh" (sparks of the spirit), and "Nishmat kol chai" (the soul of all that lives).[23] Falk cautions against using any one term to generically replace all references to God because a single term assumes absolute authority, to the exclusion of all other possible perceptions of the divine.[24] I agree with her. Throughout *Diaspora Journey,* I use many different expressions to communicate the concept of the divine spirit. My goal is not to eliminate or nullify gender. I have chosen language to express divine imagery based on many things, including the relationship of the creator to the thing created (e.g. "Sparks of the spirit," is appropriate in the context of kindling lights), and the nature of the character who speaks the words. For example, the character Mayer is the domineering patriarch of a family in 1917 Russia. When he blesses the wine, he uses, "Adonai Eloheinu, Melech Ha'olam" which is how I believe he envisions God. I think he would consider any feminine or more open expression to be inappropriate or even sacrilegious.

Preparation/Direction

In most Seders, the mother (along with other girls and women) prepares everything from the food to the house to the dishes, while the father has the most active role in performance of the Seder, taking the role of "leader" in the Haggadah. *Diaspora Journey* is designed to offer a different kind of experience. While some roles are "bigger" than others, I have not written a specific role for one leader. The real leader, therefore, is not any role within the reading of the Haggadah, but the person in charge of preparations. That person will need to determine how the table/stage will be set, what foods/props will go in what locations on the table and most importantly, which participants will play each role. In short, the preparer – traditionally a secondary role in the sociology of the home and Seder – is now the director, the primary leader.

Casting options for this Haggadah are many. Jewish tradition dictates that if one is alone for Passover, one should read the entire Haggadah himself (or herself), asking the questions and answering them.[25] If there are only two or three participants, I recommend simply alternating lines. With five or more participants, there is great potential for the Seder to communicate real connections between characters in different times by multiple-casting roles based on "The Four Children/Four Sons" from more traditional Haggadot as follows:

Miriam, Miguel, Michelle, Misha and Mila are all somehow disaffected – some, more than others (the "Wicked" child).

Moses, Maura, Mayer, Max and Present-day Marusa are all wise and/or arrogant. (The Wise Child)

Aaron, Arturo, Alexi, Asher and Alise all possess a certain open simplicity about them (The Simple Child).

Zipporah, Rosa, Pogrom-era Marusa, Elisha and Elliot are all a little lost, even while belonging with their own families (The Child Too Young To Ask).

Shira, Abuela, Elena, Lisi and Zack all have something of a sense of humor. (Not a traditional Seder archetype, but amidst the trials and adversity that the Haggadah and Seder highlight, I think it's important that at least someone be able to recognize the humor inherent in tragic situations. That ability is an important part of Jewish survival so I am adding it as a fifth, necessary, type of child.)

Directors/preparers should feel free to explore different connections between characters in different time periods. They should look for resonance between characters, then express connections with casting decisions. When I first wrote this text, present-day Marusa and Pogrom-era Marusa were the same character, written to be played by one participant. But I always knew that at some point, the dynamics of a character that existed both in a fixed place in time and a movable place in time would make Present-day Marusa impossibly old. After about ten years, I realized that it wasn't absolutely necessary to physically link those two characters in order to establish a clear connection from the past to the present. At the same time, her stories *are* related and having one person play both roles can highlight that relationship.

Since the characters, Zack, Rosa, Alexi and Asher read The Four Questions, the youngest people at the Seder should play these roles.

In the Exodus era scenes, I like the roles of "Women" and "Men" to be read by all female and male participants, respectively. There is something about hearing those male and female voices that underscores the gender-based debate in which these two groups are engaged. When a line is designated to be read by "ALL," that means that everyone at the table should read it, whether they play named characters in the scene or not. That said, I encourage directors/preparers to experiment with casting, choosing women to play male roles and vice versa.

Once casting has been established, the director must determine where to put people as well as when and how to move them around. The Haggadah contains scenes in which people must reach out to touch one another (e.g. Max and Elisha in section entitled, "Roasted Egg. Maternal/Eternal Regenerative Power. America, 1947"). Sometimes there are directions indicating that people should get up and move in the course of the Seder. Other times, it is important that people remain seated in front of their plates. Max and Elisha could be seated next to each other. Then again, because they are emotionally separated from one another until the Roasted Egg section, it might be interesting to have them seated far away from each other. Then, when Elisha tells the story of the egg, she can get up and move as she tells it – finally sitting next to Max as the story reaches its conclusion. By having her stand up to tell the story, she asserts herself physically as well as emotionally.

The traditional Haggadah states not only that it is required "to tell the story of the departure from Egypt," but that the more one tells the story, "the more praiseworthy he is."[26] Most Haggadot, therefore, encourage participants to discuss the Haggadah, departing from the text when any element of the Seder moves them to do so. While the scripted nature of Diaspora Journey might seem to prohibit such discourse, the issues raised in the play are intended to provoke additional discussion. Participants should therefore feel free to discuss their roles or any element of the play when dinner is served and at the conclusion of the play. At the director's discretion, participants may break character to ask questions or raise points for discussion during the play, as well.

The placement of all ritual food and other items is as important as the placement of scenery and props in any dramatic setting. So, for example, the participant playing Moses should be able to reach the matzohs for the section entitled, "Breaking Apart" easily. Perhaps it is less important that the participant playing Elisha be able to reach the egg if the decision is made for her to stand up and walk around to people while she is telling her story. The symbolism of each item should also be considered when setting the table/stage. Of course, stage directions and placement of people playing different characters will vary, depending on the number of people participating in the Seder performance. If appropriate, more than one Seder plate may be placed on the table(s).

Whether certain characters or all participants sing the songs that appear in the middle of the Haggadah is at the director's discretion. Personally, I like to have as many participants as possible singing, playing instruments and being a part of the music. I provide shakers and tamborines for all participants to play, which works out so well that we often wind up with a long, jingling "jam session" at the very end of the Seder. Everyone should sing at the end of the Seder. I've provided a list of suggested songs which could be sung at that point, but the list is by no means definitive or mandatory. Suffice it to say that participants should end the Seder singing whatever songs they feel moved to sing.

All participants should have the opportunity to read the Haggadah and think about the parts they will play before the Seder. The director/preparer may communicate important insights regarding the portrayal of each character but participants should be encouraged to bring their own insights to the roles. In this way, each participant brings his/her own perspective to the Seder.

Suggestions for Participants

Participants playing multiple roles should look for ways in which the characters they play are similar and different. They should also examine ways of expressing the characters' unique qualities.

When participants read as part of a group (i.e. "All" or "Women" or "Men"), they should not read in unison. Instead, each should read the line(s) as if he/she is the only one saying it. It's okay for people to finish reading the same line at different moments.

At various places in the Haggadah, text has been divided into columns. This indicates that the lines in each column are to be read simultaneously.

Above all, everyone participating in the Seder should have fun with it. Participants should look for ways to get into their roles, including coming in costume or using relevant props which are not already part of the Seder table. This Seder is dependent on individual participation. The more attention and creativity everyone brings, the better the overall experience will be for everyone.

Diaspora Journey:
A Passover Haggadah Drama

Characters:

Exodus, the Sinai
MIRIAM, a woman
MOSES, Miriam's brother
AARON, Miriam's brother
ZIPPORAH, Moses' wife
SHIRA, another woman

15th Century Spain
MIGUEL, a man
MAURA, Miguel's wife
ARTURO, Miguel's nephew
ROSA, Miguel & Maura's daughter
ABUELA, Miguel's mother

Pogrom Era Russia
MARUSA, a young girl
MAYER, Marusa's grandfather
ELENA, Marusa's mother
MISHA, Marusa's father
ALEXI, Marusa's brother

Holocaust era
MILA, a woman
LISI, Mila's sister
ELISHA, Mila's aunt
MAX, Elisha's husband
ASHER, Mila's brother

Present Day United States.
MICHELLE, an adolescent girl
ALISE, Michelle's mother
MARUSA, Michelle's grandmother
ELLIOT, Michelle's father
ZACK, Michelle's younger brother

Everyone is seated around a table(s) or, preferably, on pillows around a tablecloth (or several), festively set with places set for dinner for each person there. Some groups may want to set an extra place for Elijiah. Two candles and a Seder plate should be in the middle. There should also be a cup filled with wine (Elijiah's cup) and a cup filled with water (Miriam's cup) in the middle of the table. If you have many participants, you may want to include multiple Seder plates and pairs of candles. Otherwise, the matzah should be within reach of the person playing MOSES, Elijiah's cup should be within reach of the person playing ELISHA, Miriam's cup should be within reach of the person playing MIRIAM and the candles should be within reach of the person playing MILA. The rest of the Seder plate should be within reach of all the characters in the Present Day United States family. In front of each person, there should be a small bowl of salt water. There should be enough parsley, horseradish and charoset for everyone to eat, when the time comes to do so in the Seder.

The Seder plate should contain:
Three whole pieces of matzah, wrapped in a matzah cover or large napkin
A roasted egg
Charoset
A Horseradish root
A roasted shankbone from a lamb (or, for vegetarian seders, a roasted beet)[1]
Parsley
An orange

---

[1] Rabbi Huna in the Talmud, *Pesachim* 114b.

(Each of four participants take an end of a sheet and hold it up over everyone else, as if to form a tent.)

MILA

There was a time when you were not a slave, remember that.

MIRIAM

You walked alone, full of laughter, you bathed bare-bellied.

ASHER

You may have lost all recollection of it, remember...

MICHELLE

You say there are not words to describe it.

MIGUEL

You say it does not exist, but remember. Make an effort to remember,

MIRIAM

Or, failing that, invent.[2] It was cold and dark, during our first nights out of Egypt. We huddled under tents, away from everything that was familiar.

MARUSA

Our fear excitement and determination to step forward, away from slavery, were so strong. We never imagined how far away it all might seem to us.

MICHELLE

Listen.

MIGUEL

The winds are blowing. Remember what it felt like to have the sand shift beneath your feet as the nightwind swept up outside the tent.

(Mila lights the candles as she speaks)

MILA

נבקש השכינה נצוצת הפנש

N'VAKEYSH HASHEKHINAH, NITZOTZOT HANEFESH

Let us seek the One who dwells in our midst, the spark of our spirit. You live in this tent of our history. We see you in its intimacy. Tonight [and especially on this Shabbat][3] You call to us, we call to you, Come home.[4]

---

[2]Monique Wittig, *Les Guerilleres* (New York: Avon Books, 1973), 89 as quoted in Judith Plaskow, *Standing Again at Sinai* (San Francisco: HarperCollins, 1990), 56.

[3]Words found in brackets referencing Shabbat should be read only if the Seder is held on a Friday night.

[4]The SHEKHINAH is described as being present in tents, in homes, and in places of greatest intimacy. For more extensive explanations of the concept of SHEKHINAH as described in the Zohar, see Plaskow, 139 and Judith S. Antonelli, *In The Image of God: A Feminist Commentary on the Torah* (New Jersey: Jason Aronson, Inc., 1995), 168.

Let Us Seek the Spark
Pesach Candle Lighting Song

Corey-Jan Albert

The tent is brought down behind the participants.

The Four Questions[5]
All Times and Places

ZACK, ROSA, ALEXI and ASHER

מה נשתנה הלילה הזה מכל הלילות?

MA NISHTANA HALAILA HAZEH MIKOL HALEILOT?

שבכל הלילות אנו אוכלין חמץ ומצה, הלילה הזה כלו מצה

SHEB'CHOL HALEILOT ANU OCHLEEN CHAMEITZ UMATZAH HALAILA HAZEH KULO MATZAH

שבכל הלילות אנו אוכלין שאר ירקות, הלילה הזה מרור

SHEB'CHOL HALEILOT ANU OCHLEEN SH'AHR Y'RAKOT HALAILA HAZEH MAROR

שבכל הלילות אין אנו מטבילין אפילו פעם אחת, הלילה הזה שתי פעמים

SHEB'CHOL HALEILOT EIN ANU MATBILEEN A FEELU PA-AM ECHOD, HALAILA HAZEH SH'TAY P'AHMEEM

שבכל הלילות אנו אוכלין בין יושבין ובין מסבין, הלילה הזה כלנו מסבין

SHEB'CHOL HALEILOT ANU OCHLEEN BEIN YOSHVEEN UVEIN M'SUBEEN, HALAILA HAZEH KULAHNU M'SUBEEN

USA, The Present

ZACK

Why is this night different from all other nights? On all other nights, we may eat either leavened or unleavened bread; why do we eat only matzah and no bread on this night? On all other nights we may eat any kinds of herbs; why on this night only bitter herbs? On all other nights we do not dip even once; why on this night do we dip twice? On all other nights we eat and drink either sitting or reclining; why on this night do we recline?

ELLIOT

Great job, Zack. (Pause) Michelle?

MICHELLE

Yeah, yeah, great job.

(Michelle is staring off into space)

ELLIOT

Michelle, wake up!

MICHELLE

(very fast, bored, and as if she is skipping words) Okay, okay. We eat matzah because our ancestors didn't have time for the bread to rise, so we baked matzah to take with us out of Egypt. We eat bitter herbs to remind us of how bitter our lives were when we were slaves. We dip our food in salt water to remind us of tears we cried and the sea we crossed. We recline because we aren't slaves anymore.

---

[5]Interestingly, most Haggadot translate the word קושיות (KUSHIYOT), as "questions," and indeed, many rephrase the text (as I have in the English translation) so that the points made in this section can be punctuated as questions. However, the actual Hebrew word for "questions" is שאלות (SHE'ELOT). The word קושיות actually translates to "difficulties" or "objections." I believe that the difference is significant: questions require answers - yes or no, right or wrong. Objections or difficulties are more like issues that need to be discussed and addressed, as we do in the Passover Seder.

MARUSA

How are we supposed to understand when she goes so fast?

ALISE

Michelle?

MICHELLE

Well, none of us were ever slaves. We weren't. We've always lived right here in America. Land of the free. So why talk as if we were?

ALISE

Our family didn't always live here.

MARUSA

Oh yes, the stories I could tell you about our family back in Russia...

MICHELLE

But no one in our family ever lived in Egypt did they?

MARUSA

Back in Russia, some of it was worse than Egypt.

MICHELLE

How was it worse?

ELLIOT

Michelle. Enough. We don't want to be here all night.

MICHELLE

Forget I asked, then. I mean, it's not like we're supposed to ask questions, right? Why is this night different from any other night? Matzah, herbs, dipping, reclining. I'd rather hear Grandma's stories. We can read about Pharoah and Moses any time. The whole thing is all about a bunch of men none of us ever knew anyway.

ALISE

Michelle, it wasn't all only about men.

MICHELLE

Yeah? How do you know?

First Cup of Wine: Forgetting.

MARUSA

You know, when I was a girl, I remember –

ELLIOT

Grandma –

MARUSA

I remember that we used to mind our elders. (Pause.) Thank you. I was just going to say about when Zaide used to say the blessings – do you remember? He'd have this big booming voice.

ELLIOT

My grandfather? A big booming voice? Grandpa had a little quiet voice.

MARUSA

Oh no, he'd call out those bruchas so that just in case God was at the Seder next door, he'd hear.

ELLIOT

Mom, you're confused.

ZACK

Dad, just leave her alone.

ELLIOT

Zack —

MARUSA

No, no, I'm not confused. It's you. You've forgotten.

ELLIOT

Mom, you are confused. I haven't forgotten because I wasn't there. Grandpa was an old man by the time I knew him. Don't you remember?

(Marusa realizes that nobody else *does* remember what she does, and sighs).

MARUSA

I suppose I don't. My memory isn't what it once was.

ELLIOT

(A little exasperated) Mom, your memory was never what it once was. You've always had a terrible memory.

ALISE

She can remember things from fifty years ago, but she can't remember what she did this morning. Why does that happen?

MARUSA

I don't know. Why is it that when you get old, people talk about you like you're not right there in the room with them.

ALISE

I didn't mean – I'm sorry.

MICHELLE

Maybe it's the wine.

ALISE

What?

ZACK

Leave it to Michelle.

MICHELLE

Oh yeah. And you know it all. I'm only saying that four cups of wine is a lot. If we really drank the whole cup instead of taking a little sip, I think we'd all forget a lot of things.

ALISE

Michelle. It's a ceremony. Not a bacchanalia. Besides, how would you know about how much wine would make you forget things?

ZACK

Yeah, Michelle. How would you know?

MICHELLE

(whining/exasperated) Mom...

ALISE

(imitating) Mom... I'm only asking.

ZACK

She's only asking.

MICHELLE

Stop it, Zack. Mom, make him stop.

ALISE

Zack, cut it out.

MICHELLE

Everyone knows what alcohol can do to people. Everyone who reads anything.

ELLIOT

And what's that supposed to mean?

MICHELLE

(sullen) Nothing. It doesn't mean anything.

ELLIOT

Michelle. Please. It's a Seder. And I'd appreciate it if you were here with the rest of us.

MICHELLE

What? I didn't say anything except that maybe wine can make people forget things.

ALISE

That's right. It can. In excess. But maybe wine symbolizes creativity, too. You crush the grapes and they turn into something else... And bread, bread is creative too. Bread is all about nurturing. And Matzah especially – very creative solution to the problem of what food to pack when you're in a hurry.

ELLIOT

So what's the creative solution to eating Matzah for a whole week solid?

MARUSA

Prunes, Elliot. (Pause) Well, at least I remember one thing.

ALISE

You want to know what I think, Mom? I think that life fills us up with so many experiences. So much history. You have to make room for the important memories. So, it's not important that you remember what you ate for breakfast yesterday.

MARUSA

I think that when I remember when terrible things have happened, I'd rather forget.

ALISE

Was your breakfast yesterday so awful?

MARUSA

I think I had some toast. And a banana. It was going bad. See, so I'm not so crazy.

ELLIOT

Mom, nobody said you were crazy.

MARUSA

Oh, no, but you think it. I know—

MICHELLE

Grandma, tell us about when you were a little girl.

ELLIOT

Michelle, don't get her started.

MICHELLE

I want to hear it.

8

ZACK

Yeah, Dad.

ELLIOT

Okay, here we go. When I was a girl...

MARUSA

When I was a girl, every Passover, they'd tell stories of that one Passover back in Russia. Oh, some of those stories were... sad and frightening and terrible -- and wonderful. They gave me terrible nightmares, but even so, I loved those stories, especially because there was a little girl in the stories named Marusa. I never met her, of course, she was dead when I was born. But I was named for her, so I always felt an affinity – Oh, what am I saying? You know all this. I've told you before.

(she pauses - everyone is listening)

All right, then. So, they'd start the story with Mayer, the great patriarch at the head of the table. The rest of the year, everyone was a little frightened of him. But on Passover... that was different. Well, mostly different. They said that he called out the blessing with such power —

(Everyone raises a glass)

MAYER

ברוך אתה יי אלהינו מלך העולם. בורא פרי הגפן.
BARUCH ATA ADONAI, ELOHEINU MELECH HA-OLAM. BOREH P'RI HAGAFEN

MARUSA

Blessed art thou, Lord our God, Creator of the fruit of the vine. My brothers and I, we would sit up, still. As if his voice was in the room with us. We'd hold up our wine glasses. They were made of beautiful crystal, you can't get crystal like that now. It was so light that you could actually feel the sound of the voices echoing. Shush for a minute and listen. That's the way. Then lean back, put the glass up to your lips. Can you still feel the words ringing there? I remember. It was like drinking the wine and the blessing together, at the same time.

(Everyone drinks)

9

Russia, 1917.

ELENA

Marusa? Stop daydreaming.

MARUSA

I wasn't, Mama, I was just —

MAYER

Very well, then. Now, we come to the —

MISHA

Papa – shh – did you hear that?

MAYER

(Clears throat) Again. Now we come to the —

MISHA

There. There it was again. Outside. Hooves.

MAYER

Here it is, a holy ceremony, and all my son can imagine is that soldiers will come marauding through the house.

ALEXI

Mama, do you really think that the soldiers will come?

ELENA

See, Misha, you're frightening the children.

MISHA

Well, maybe they should be a little frightened. The Tsar's soldiers could come galloping through the streets at any time.

MARUSA

Look what they did to Giorgyi's shop.

ELENA

Giorgyi taunts the soldiers every day. He dares them to do something. If I were a soldier, I'd try to teach Giorgyi a lesson, too.

MAYER

Giorgyi is a baker. And he's not so big. What could a little baker do? Knead them to death? Ha ha.

ELENA

Giorgyi is a trouble maker. I don't know how his wife puts up with him.

ALEXI

How his wife puts up with him? How does Giorgyi put up with his wife?

MISHA

Alexi!

ALEXI

What? I think Giorgyi doesn't have any choice. His wife is bigger than he is.

MISHA

It isn't nice to speak of others that way, when they're not here.

ALEXI

But it's true. She is bigger. I saw that they broke all his windows. (To Marusa, teasing) Maybe there's broken glass in the matzohs.

MARUSA

(gasps) What if there is?

MAYER

Children, children, there is no glass in the matzohs.

MISHA

Giorgyi's wife ate all those pieces.

ELENA

She should only hear you.

MAYER

She can't hear you. The soldiers can't hear me. There is nothing to be afraid of. Now, Marusa, Alexi, please get the water.

(Marusa and Alexi get the pitcher of water, a towel and a bowl. One of them pours the water over Mayer's hands. The pitcher and bowl are then passed to the left. Each person pours water over the hands of the person to his/her left, going around the table, while the reading continues. For convenience/expedience, more than one pitcher may be used)

MARUSA

The sound of the water was magic, washing away everything else. We forgot that soldiers could gallop through the streets and overtake our homes. We forgot that the water was in pitchers and bowls.

11

Water and Greens
The Desert, Time of Exodus

MIRIAM
It is the water of the Red Sea that drowned the Egyptians chasing us. It is the water in Marah, where we arrived after three days of wandering with no water at all. We are in the desert. Thirsty. Tired. And this is the only water for miles.

SHIRA
Was it really so bad in Egypt? We had shelter. We had beds at night. We had water to drink.

ZIPPORAH
Laced with our sweat and blood.

SHIRA
This water is laced with more than that. Have you tasted it?

AARON
That's because it's our history. All the things we're forgetting. Catching up to us to remind us of how the Egyptians made our lives so hard and bitter.

MIRIAM
And now, what are our lives like now, Aaron? We've wandered for three days with no water.

SHIRA
There is still water in Egypt. All right, so it wasn't our ancestors' home. But it's the only home we ever knew. Aaron, Miriam, Moses – what have we done?

ZIPPORAH
Listen to yourselves! We had backbreaking labor.

WOMEN
Pain!

MEN
Humiliation!

ZIPPORAH
We had fear beyond belief.

SHIRA
Oh, and no one is scared now. Look at us. We're parched and dry. Drained. And there is nothing ahead of us. Nothing.

ZIPPORAH
So, this water is filled with all the bitterness we've forgotten. And none of us wants to dare drink it.

SHIRA
Tell me about it. We *should* forget all that we've suffered. I don't *ever* want to think back on it again.

MIRIAM

You don't want to think back on our past? Three days ago we were dancing for joy at our escape. That's our past too, now.

SHIRA

The children have nightmares. They wake up crying.

ZIPPORAH

They wake up! For the longest time, the nightmare was real.

MOSES

Yes! Look around you. Things grow here. *We* can grow here. We're learning not to cringe when someone startles us, afraid that we'll be dragged away in our sleep.

SHIRA

The children are thirsty.

ALL

All of us are thirsty.

AARON

Then drink. Drink this water.

SHIRA

How?

MOSES

(Holding up greens) Look at this. It grows here with strong roots. Without drinking the water of history, there is no home to return to, nothing to guide us. Escape our bitter past. Yes. But if we do not drink our history, we will scatter apart like feathers and dust.

AARON

Children born from now on will never know what we've been through. And when you tell them about it, they won't believe you – unless it remains part of you. Drink your history and you will pass it on to your children. Spit out your history and there is nothing to keep them safe from its legacy.

MIRIAM

Look. Dip this into the water. Taste something that grows from it and you will be able to stand the bitterness of this history, this water.

(Everyone dips the greens into the salt water)

AARON

נברך את מקור החיים בורא פרי האדמה.
N'VAREYKH ET MAKOR HACHAYIM BOREH P'RI HA-ADAMA.

MOSES

Let us bless the source of life that brings forth the fruit of the earth.

(everyone eats the greens)

Think back. It was just a few days ago. Late in the day. We arrived at the Sea of Reeds. Pharaoh had just learned that the people had fled and he was angry. "What is this we have done, releasing Israel from our service?" he demanded. He led all of his warriors, all the horses and chariots to chase after us. We heard the sound of galloping hooves and rumbling wheels before we caught the terrifying sight of the Egyptians advancing, faster and faster.

SHIRA

Why were we brought here? To make sure we had graves *outside* of Egypt? We told you it would come to this. "It is better for us to serve the Egyptians than to die in the wilderness!" we said. But Did Moses listen? We followed you! And this is where you lead us? We must have been crazy!

ZIPPORAH

No. Not madness. Desperation.

MOSES

Stand up. Get ready.

SHIRA

For what? So that Pharaoh's soldiers can see us better?

MIRIAM

We did not come all this way to have it end with our children's blood on Pharaoh's swords.

SHIRA

We didn't come to drown ourselves, either.

AARON

Have no fear!

MIRIAM

(gently) A little late for that, don't you think?

AARON

Stand by and witness the deliverance which ADONAI will work for you today.

(All except Moses, Aaron & Miriam speak one of the following sentences, simultaneously)

ALL (say just one of the phrases below – your choice)

I can't look./I can't believe./I can't breathe.

MOSES

You must.

AARON

Yes! Look closely. The Egyptians whom you see today, you will never see again.

MOSES

(Under his breath) Dear God, they are still advancing. Yet you say have no fear and reach out across the water. And still they come.

(Picks up the middle matzah from the stack and holds it with two outstretched hands in front of him)

15

MOSES

Go forward!

(Breaks the middle matzah in two, creating the Afikoman, the piece of Matzah saved for the end of the meal)

And we went into the sea on dry ground, surrounded by walls of water.

(Moses wraps the larger half of the Afikoman in a napkin; at some point during the Seder, by the end of dinner, the participant playing Moses must secretly hide the Afikoman somewhere in the room)

MIRIAM'S SONG

Spain, 1491[6]

MIGUEL

Lo! This is the bread of affliction which our fathers ate in the land of Egypt.

MAURA

Let all who are hungry come and eat. Let all who are in want come and celebrate the Passover with us. This year we are here. Next year we shall be in the land of Israel. This year we are in servitude. Next year we shall be free.

MIGUEL

Freedom, freedom. What is freedom anyway? Lonely and isolated and lost. The Israelites had no choice. And they had Moses. This is different. This is 1491 Spain.

MAURA

1491. Modern Spain. What does that mean? What guarantees do any of us have? We must be like the Israelites. Ferdinand and Isabela have the evil eye on us. We must leave Spain. Now. Before the real terror begins.

MIGUEL

And go where? East? To Egypt? Ferdinand and Isabela will not touch us. We are their bankers. We are their advisors. They need us. This is our home.

MAURA

Well, it always was. But when I look around us... everything is changing.

MIGUEL

Everything is always changing.

MAURA

Yes, yes, but this is different. And it's all in the little things. Even with neighbors who always seemed to like us.

MIGUEL

Did somebody say something to you?

ABUELA

Nobody has to. They would never *say* anything to our faces. But no one wants to be seen too close to us either.

MAURA

It's heartbreaking, Miguel.

---

[6] A note on pronunciation for those who do not speak any Spanish: Miguel is "Mee-GAYL," Maura is "MAO-rah," Abuela is "A-BWAY-la," Jesús is "Hay-SOOS," bueno is "BWAY-no," madre is "MAH-dray" and "hija" is "EE-cha" (with the "ch" pronounced as the gutteral throat-clearing sound at the beginning of "Chanukah" or the end of "Bach.")

MIGUEL

(sigh) Always so sensitive.

MAURA

I'm telling you. This is something else. This is different.

MIGUEL

You listen to too many old women.

ABUELA

Old women? You listen to this old woman. I will tell you. You sit here and argue but all around us, this *is* Egypt. But you cannot see anything. You just talk talk talk. You'll still be talking when the soldiers come after your children with swords.

MIGUEL

(To Maura) You see?

ROSA

(to Maura) Mama!

MAURA

(To Abuela) Mama! You're scaring the children!

ABUELA

Good! They need to be scared. All of you. You need to be scared. You tell the Haggadah as if it were a bedtime story. It's not just a story. It's real.

MIGUEL

I won't have this at my Seder table. As for me, I believe we can stay.

MAURA

No, we can't.

MIGUEL

What? No, of course we can. You don't know what you're saying, Maura.

MAURA

I know exactly what I'm saying, Miguel. We have only one choice. And that is to go.

MIGUEL

Go. Go. Go where? Do you take your chances and sail to some new world? With Cristobal Colon the madman?

ARTURO

It would be fun to sail on a ship.

MIGUEL

Shh. We're not going on any ship. Your parents would never allow it. (To Abuela) Can you just imagine Rebecca's face, Mama?

18

ABUELA

You do not give your sister enough credit. I did not raise my children to be fools. At least I thought I
didn't. Listen to yourself, Miguel. Do you hear how preposterous your words are?

ARTURO

My mama and papa would let me sail on a ship.

ABUELA

Hush, little one.

MAURA

Where then? Do we go east? Do we sneak into France? The French have no love for us.

MIGUEL

This is so unnecessary. We can stay. We will simply be Jewish in secret.

MAURA

Secret? How long will anything remain a secret with so many babbling fools around?

ABUELA

Amen.

MIGUEL

It will be secret.

MAURA

Oh? And when the Soldiers come and tell us to swear loyalty to *Jesús*, you will do it?

MIGUEL

I'll say what they want. They won't know the difference.

MAURA

And you? Will you know the difference? Or will it just be easier to convert.

MIGUEL

My tongue cannot betray my heart to them.

ABUELA

Your tongue will be the death of you fools.

ARTURO

I will be a great sailor – on a great adventure!

ROSA

Will Moses be there? Will he part the sea?

(Note: sections of dialogue presented side by side in two or more columns are meant to be read simultaneously)

ARTURO

Rosa, imagine it. We'll be on a great ship, sailing to find riches and new places. It will be a great adventure.

ROSA

You get seasick just looking at the ocean.

ARTURO

I do not. Abuela, tell her. Tell her about being on a ship. You know all about it.

ABUELA

That was a long time ago. I do not know that the ship is our answer.

ARTURO

Abuela...

ROSA

What is it like, Abuela? Tell us.

ABUELA

A ship. Well, it's wet. And it's noisy. And you do get seasick. And the sailors stink of dirt and –

ARTURO

See? It will be great, Rosa. You'll see!

MIGUEL

We must stay. To leave will be death.

MAURA

You really believe the terror will pass.

MIGUEL

Of course it will. You tell them what they want to hear. You bend a little. Let the storm pass. And it does. And you stand up again.

MAURA

As a Christian or a Jew?

MIGUEL

As a man. A living, breathing man.

ABUELA

Here, at this Seder, you have the chutzpah to swear loyalty to the people who would kill your father? Or your wife?

MIGUEL

We could just tell them we're *conversos*. Let them spill water on our heads. We'll know what we believe. Who else will know?

MAURA

They'll know. We can't hide.

ABUELA	ARTURO	MAURA	MIGUEL
They don't know what they are saying. Colon and his men will cast us over the side as soon as the waters get rough. He only needs our money. Once he has that, we're useless to him. Colon is not our savior. He isn't even our Moses! He is a crazy, ambitious man, with lust for gold, and who knows what else. Ai, Miguel, you talk of keeping secrets as if it were as easy. It's men who have to brag to each other about everything. Feh. The way your father talked in his sleep, it was lucky for him I already knew all his secrets.	Imagine it. We will sail through the wind and the rain, fearless! Just think of it! We *will* be like the Israelites. The sea will part for our boat as we sail onto the future. Oh, if Mama and Papa were here, they would want to go. But Papa and Mama are still away on Papa's business. I thought they'd be home by now. But I just know it – when they return, we will sail away. They'll have to say yes! I wonder if I'll get to have a sword. Yes! I will! If Papa were here, he would convince them all, I know he would.	(Sigh) Miguel, I love you. You know that I will follow you anywhere, even if anywhere is only here – but listen to yourself! It is madness to stay where we are so unwelcome. How will we survive if you forsake everything you've ever believed? But maybe we go east like your sister and her husband... (sigh) Listen to Arturo. When will we tell him? They said they would send for Arturo. Do you believe they will? Will we all escape into the desert like the Hebrews?	We can hide. If we light candles on a Friday night, who's to stop us? Lots of people light candles in the darkness. My mother said it: This is reality. And in our reality, we must survive. Listen to me. Who cares what anyone else calls me, what words I recite? They're just words. Is it better for us to go off into oblivion like my sister? They did not want to bring hardship upon their son. And I will not go against their wishes. Or my own heart. Our lives are here. Not on the sea or in the desert.

ROSA

(just before they all get to the end of their lines) Stop it! Just stop it! All of you are talking. None of you are listening. You don't care that we'll never see each other again!

Second Cup of Wine: Remembering
USA, 1947.

MILA

I thought we'd never see each other again. As we sit here, at this Passover, I am overwhelmed... that we are... here together. I only wish Papa could have been alive to see this.

LISI

Mama... would have loved to see this.

MILA

I tried to find her, Lisi, I did. So many records were... missing.

MAX

The Nazis kept meticulous records. So proud of what they had done. They didn't want to leave out a single detail.

MILA

Well, somebody realized that the records might be found. Some... whole groups of them were all destroyed. I remember when Papa and I came to America, he knew what was happening. What was going to happen. He never forgave himself for going ahead with just me. He was always... just a fraction of himself, missing Mama. Missing all of you.

LISI

Mila, none of us could have known that it would happen so fast.

MAX

I don't suppose it ever occurred to him that your mother and the rest of us wouldn't be along just a few months later. He knew that Hitler would reign in terror. He thought he was getting everyone out soon enough.

MILA

He thought he was being so smart by not telling anyone what he was doing. He didn't want anyone to slip and talk about it. He thought it would be a great surprise. For us to wire everyone and say, "We're here in America! Come to us!"

MAX

That was Joseph, all right. Always the dreamer. Always the drama...

MILA

We set up this house as if everyone would be here soon. Then we had trouble reaching you. Then we started to hear. Slowly at first. Papa knew early on. But he didn't tell me until people really started talking about it.

MAX

Hmmph. If only we could have been a better subject for gossip.

MILA

Well, it was so frightening. So incredible. Nobody wanted to believe it.

LISI

(changing the subject) Mila. Do you remember that Passover with the kitten and the wine?

ASHER

What kitten?

LISI

That kitten we had. Mimi. You remember. That Passover when we couldn't find her? And then, bloop, bloop, bloop, we found footsteps made of wine, leading right from the kitchen, all over the house, finally on your bed, licking her paws?

MILA

I don't think the stains ever came off.

ASHER

I don't remember that at all.

MILA

Oh, right. It broke up the whole Seder.

ASHER

Well, I really don't remember.

MILA

Mimi was drunk with all that wine on her paws. Come on, Asher, how can you not remember?

LISI

She'd be gone for days at a time, then she'd come home like nothing ever happened and she'd always come lie down on your head, Asher.

ASHER

No, no. It wasn't like that at all.

LISI

Don't you remember, you were afraid of the cat. Always. If I ever wanted to scare you, all I'd have to do was go [low purring noise].

ASHER

You're crazy. I was never afraid of cats.

LISI

Yes you were.

ASHER

Well, I like cats now.

(Lisi makes a low purring noise)

ASHER

Stop it, Lisi!

LISI

See?

ASHER

No, it has nothing to do with that. You're just always telling me how I'm supposed to remember things. And they're not that way at all.

MILA

How would you know? You can never remember anything.

ELISHA

I remember when they first brought you to Auschwitz, Mila. I could hardly recognize you with all your hair gone. But I knew.

MAX

(gently) Mila never went to Auschwitz. She was in America. You know that.

ELISHA

Oh. Yes, of course. You're right.

MAX

Yes I am. *I* know. *I* was there. I was there for them smashing our homes, destroying glasses, dishes, windows, art... I was there in the trains where we were packed like cargo, where a woman fell dead beside me – and couldn't even lie down because there was no room. I rode with her like that, cold and dead beside me, stinking of disease. I was there when the Nazis —

ASHER

Uncle Max!

MAX

I was there when they made us choose between —

LISI

Stop it, Uncle Max!!

MAX

– Our two children, right in front of them.

LISI

Uncle Max – don't do this!

MAX

(cold. calm.) And I was there when they killed them both anyway and dragged us off to —

MILA

Oh my G- -- No!

MAX

You have to remember it, Elisha!!

MILA

How could – I can't – Oh, Aunt Elisha.

ELISHA

What? Anna and Maike, they escaped. I know they did.

(Max just burries his face in his hands)

We couldn't watch.

MILA

Could it be possible, Uncle Max?

MAX

What do you think?

LISI

Uncle Max. Let her be. What good will it do to make her –

MAX

I can't bear it. For her to be this way.

MILA

I know.

MAX

No, that's just it! You don't know.

MILA

(lost. Trying to change the subject) You can't imagine what it was like when we —

MAX

I can't imagine? No, it's you who can't imagine, Mila. You weren't there. Not for any of it.

LISI

Uncle Max, leave her alone!

MILA

(hurt, but still trying) ... when we started to realize that you really weren't coming. Suddenly, this house was enormous and empty. This table was so big. Papa and I never ate here. We would sit at that little table in the kitchen. But now... look at us. (Takes out a photo) Look at this. It's so ragged now. But look. That's all of us. Passover 1937... Now look around this table. Passover 1947. So let's have a toast.

(All raise glasses)

MILA

To our family.

MAX

To what we have lost.

LISI

To our survival.

ASHER

To our future.

MAX

ברוך אתה יי אלהינו מלך העולם. בורא פרי הגפן.

BARUCH ATA ADONAI, ELOHEINU MELECH HA-OLAM. BOREH P'RI HAGAFEN.

(All drink the second cup of wine)

The Ten Plagues/Dayenu/Bread and Sustenance
Spain, 1493

MIGUEL

(rushing) Now, we pour ten drops for the plagues upon Egypt. Blood, Frogs, lice, beasts, blight, boils, hail, locusts, darkness, slaying of the first —

ROSA

Papa! You're going too fast.

ABUELA

He's trying to race so he can make it to the church.

MAURA

(shocked) Tonight, Miguel? Tonight? On Pesach, you would do this?

MIGUEL

This close to Easter? Yes. I would do this. I would do this because it has kept you alive, my family.

ARTURO

I want to go with Tio Miguel.

MIGUEL

Sí, of course, you may come with me Arturo.

ARTURO

Bueno, bueno!

MAURA

Arturo, no! I won't have it!

ABUELA

Miguel! Are you insane?!

MIGUEL

No, it is *you* who are insane, Mama! All of our friends are at the church – and they'll stay our friends so long as we join them there.

ABUELA

Our friends and family are either on a boat to the Indies or traveling east to the promised land. Or dead, like your brother Avram at the hands of —

MIGUEL

Count your blessings, Abuela! We are alive. We have not lost our homes. We are respected in our community.

MAURA

And we live in fear. Miguel, look at what's happened to you. I agreed to this... to stay... because you promised we would keep our identity.

27

That is the only reason why you stayed?

MAURA

(pause) Miguel. I could never leave you. But this. Every time something happens, we can rationalize. "That would be enough." Everything is "*Dayenu*."

ALL

Dayenu!

Dayenu

Trad.

I-lu-natan, Na-tan La-nu,
Na-tan La-nu et Ha-sha-bat,
Na-tan La-nu et Ha-sha-bat
Dayenu (Chorus)

I-lu Na-tan, Na-tan La-nu,
Na-tan La-nu et Ha-to-rah
Na-tan La-nu et Ha-to-rah
Dayenu (Chorus)

MAURA

If we had stayed in hiding but kept our identities...

ALL

Dayenu!

MAURA

...it would have been enough. If we had lost our homes, but kept our self respect...

ALL

Dayenu!

MAURA

If we had lost our homes and been thrown into jail...

ALL

Dayenu!

MAURA

If we —

MIGUEL

Dayenu. Dayenu. Where would it end? If we lost our lives? Dayenu then, Maura? Really?

MAURA

Miguel, it's just that – to see you race through the Seder this way – so you can leave to go to – This is too much of a sacrifice. Look at Arturo and how he looks up to you. Would Rebecca and Eduardo want him raised like this?

MIGUEL

Do not mock my loyalty to my sister and her husband. They trusted us to keep their son safe. That is exactly what we are doing. We were never very religious before, Maura.

ABUELA

It was never this important before. It's important now.

MIGUEL

Important? Important? Let me tell you what's important. You think that the church officials do not know what night this is? If I am late to their meeting, I will draw suspicion to our house. I'll make it up to you, *preciosa*, I will. Believe me, I know what I'm doing. Arturo, come with me. Let's go.

(Arturo and Miguel turn away from the table)

MAURA

(takes a deep breath) So. *Madre. Hija*. It comes down to us three. We diminish the cup of joy by ten drops for the plagues upon Egypt.

ABUELA

The plagues upon us all.

(Everyone dips a finger into the wine to pour ten drops)

ABUELA

דם Dam.

ROSA

Blood.

29

                              MAURA

The blood of loved ones, family we hardly knew, splashed against the earth because they were proud to be who they were.

                              ABUELA

צפרדע Tsfardeya.

                              ROSA

Frogs

                              MAURA

We smile like frogs, fearing the frown, hopping and falling, squatting for so long that we have no size.[7]

                              ABUELA

כנים Kinim.

                              ROSA

Lice.

                              MAURA

We are the insects. Insignificant as long as we are invisible.

                              ABUELA

ערוב Arov.

                              ROSA

Wild Beasts

                              MAURA

They pretend to be gentle as they circle around us, pacing, waiting. They will be patient until we make a mistake. Then they tear our souls from our bodies.

                              ABUELA

דבר Dever.

                              ROSA

Blight.

                              MAURA

It is a disease upon us. To turn away from our history. To be blind to our legacy. To give in to the fear. To embrace the safe and the convenient.

                              ABUELA

שחין Sh'chin.

                              ROSA

Boils.

---

[7]Paraphrased from E.M. Broner, *The Telling* (San Francisco: HarperCollins, 1992) 208.

MAURA

It festers. The true nature under the false skin.

ABUELA

ברד Barad.

ROSA

Hail.

MAURA

Always say what they want to hear. Never let the tears melt and fall down like gentle rain.

ABUELA

ארבה Arbeh.

ROSA

Locusts.

MAURA

They swarm about us to devour... destroy... then leave us as they fly away.

ABUELA

חשך Choshech.

ROSA

Darkness.

MAURA

Hide our candles in the darkest corners of our houses. Where they cannot be seen. Where they will never be recognized.

ABUELA

מכת בכורות Makat B'chorot.

ROSA

Slaying of the First Born.

(Silence)

Mama? Will they be all right?

ABUELA

My first born. . . And the first born of my daughter . . . are wandering, lost among those who would never save them. God, please, do not forsake them.

MAURA

Amen. Now let us wash the wine of our fingers. Wash the plagues away.

(Again, each person pours water over the hands of the person to her/his left. Once everyone has washed hands, Abuela holds up a piece of Matzah)

ABUELA

This is the bread of affliction which our ancestors ate in the land of Egypt. Let all who are hungry come and eat. Whoever is in need come and celebrate the Passover. Now here.

ROSA

Next year in the land of Israel.

MAURA

Now enslaved.

ROSA

Next year, children of freedom.

MAURA

ברוך אתה יי אלהינו מלך העולם. המוציא לחם מן-הארץ

BARUCH ATA ADONAI, ELOHEINU MELECH HA-OLAM. HAMOTZI LECHEM MIN HA ORETZ.

Blessed are you, oh Lord our God, King of the Universe, who brings forth bread from the earth.

ברוך אתה יי אלהינו מלך העולם. אשר קדשנו במצותיו וצונו על-אכילת מצה

BARUCH ATA ADONAI, ELOHEINU MELECH HA-OLAM. ASHER KIDSHANU, B'MITZVO-TAV, V'TZIVANU, AL ACHILAT MATZAH.

Blessed are you, oh Lord our God, King of the universe who has commanded us to eat Matzah.

(everyone eats some matzah Abuela takes the bowl of water, walks to the door of the house (preferably a back door), opens it and throws the water outside).

ABUELA

Muchos años, everyone. Long lives to us all.[8]

ALL

Muchos años!

(Abuela comes back inside and firmly shuts the door behind her)

MAURA

God only knows what the future will bring.

---

[8]It is a Sephardic tradition to throw the water used for hand washing out the door, followed by the statement, "*Muchos Años*," (literally, "Many years"). Ruth Gruber Fredman, *The Passover Seder: Afikoman in Exile* (Philadelphia: University of Pennsylvania Press, 1981) 107-108.

Bones
USA, The Present.

ELLIOT

Rabban Gamaliel said: "Whoever does not mention the meaning of these three symbols, the Paschal lamb, the unleavened bread and the bitter herbs, has not fulfilled his obligation."

MICHELLE

What about her obligation?

ELLIOT

Michelle.

(Points to the shankbone)

This Passover sacrifice which our fathers used to eat at the time when the Holy Temple still stood.

MICHELLE

Ugh.

ALISE

Michelle. Please.

MICHELLE

I can't help it. Meat is barbaric.

(Zack picks up the bone and waves it at Michelle)

ZACK

Mmmmm....meat!

MICHELLE

Gross.

ALISE

Zack, put it down.

(Zack puts the bone back)

Michelle. Nobody said you had to eat it. I made plenty of vegetables for you to eat tonight. The lamb is just what our ancestors ate.

MICHELLE

It's disgusting.

MARUSA

What is this? You always loved lamb chops.

MICHELLE

Grandma. Please. Give me a break.

ZACK

You hear that, Grandma? My stupid sister doesn't want to eat meat anymore.

MARUSA

The way your mother cooks it? *Feh*. You know what they call that? That's a *shandeh*. A shame. Now when I was growing up, that was different. My mother cooked everything until it was like your shoes.

MICHELLE

Well, leather shoes are barbaric, too.

ZACK

Mmmmm... Leather!

ALISE

Okay, both of you. That's enough. Can Dad get on with the Seder now?

ELLIOT

Thank you, Alise. Okay. This shankbone – what was the reason for it? It was because the Holy One, blessed by he, passed over the houses of our fathers in Egypt.

MICHELLE

What about our mothers? Is there a reason why there weren't any women there?

ELLIOT

Is there a reason why you keep interrupting?

MICHELLE

I'm only asking: He, His, Him.

ZACK

It's because that's the way it is. Get used to it.

ALISE

It's the way it *was*. You have to understand, Michelle. Women weren't always very well educated. There wasn't any women's liberation. Think about it. If you had been alive back then, you wouldn't go to school. In fact, at 15, you'd probably be married now, with at least a baby or two. If you had been alive back then —

MICHELLE

If I had been alive back then, I would've changed all that.

MARUSA

I bet she would have, too, Elliot. She's a smart one, your daughter.

ZACK

If you had been alive back then, you would be dead now.

34

MICHELLE

I'd be haunting you, Zack.

ALISE

And the day we see a woman on the bimah will be the day there's an orange on the Seder plate.

ELLIOT

Oh, to live in the old days, when women knew their place.

ZACK

Go Dad! Yes!

ALISE

Zack. Elliot. I'll bean you both with the orange if you don't cut it out.

ELLIOT

Kidding! I was kidding!

ZACK

Oh yeah. Me too. (Under his breath) Not.

MICHELLE

Watch it, Zack.

MARUSA

Children. It's a Seder.

MICHELLE

Grandma, it doesn't make any sense. They were wandering around in the desert. There had to be a lot of work to do. It's not like the men hunted and killed while the women tended the tent fires.

ELLIOT

Well, lots of things didn't make sense. Like 40 years in the desert. The Sinai's not *that* big. Don't you think that one day someone looked around and said, "Hey. Doesn't that big mountain look familiar?"

MICHELLE

They were supposed to be wandering around long enough for all the old people to die off.

MARUSA

Oh yes. Isn't that the way it always goes.

ALISE

Michelle!

MICHELLE

I'm sorry, Grandma. I didn't mean it like that.

MARUSA

No, no. I know. But sometimes it takes a long time for us old people to finish up our business.

MICHELLE

But that's what I mean. That's why they were wandering around for so long.

ELLIOT

You think God made them all lose their way?

MICHELLE

Well, yeah, maybe.

MARUSA

You don't think the elders realized what was going on? The truth is that they didn't want to leave their families behind in the desert. So they stuck around until they felt like their families could go on just fine without them.

MICHELLE

You mean, you think that the elders kept everyone wandering?

ALISE

It makes sense. They had to pass on everything their children might need to survive in the promised land.

MARUSA

Most of us, I think, stick around as long as we feel like somebody needs us.

ZACK

We need you, Grandma.

MICHELLE

Of course we do.

MARUSA

I'm still here, aren't I?

ELLIOT

Mom, if that's what accounts for your long life and good health, may it only be true for all of us.

ALISE

Amen.

MARUSA

Oh, so who's counting years? You know I'm not in the health I once was... sometimes I get so –

ALISE

(not about to let her get on this track) Want to know what I think?

MARUSA

(sighs.) Yes, darling, what do you think?

ALISE

Really?

ZACK

Sure, Mom.

ALISE

Everyone? You really want to know?

ELLIOT

Alise!

MICHELLE

Mom!

ALISE

Well . . . I think . . . that after 39 and a half years of aimless wandering . . . Moses' wife . . . finally . . . secretly asks for directions.

ELLIOT

That's an old joke. And I don't think it's that funny.

ALISE

Gee, I wonder why?

MARUSA

(to Alise) I think he gets that from Jake. Your grandfather could never ask for directions either, Elliot.

ELLIOT and MIRIAM *from the next section*

I don't have to take any of this from you.

Bitterness
The Desert, Time of Moses.

MIRIAM

I'm your older sister, Moses.

AARON

Aren't we beyond that now Miriam?

MIRIAM

No, Aaron. We're not beyond it. As long as he continues to act as if —

MOSES

It's all right Aaron. She doesn't bother me. There are more important things right now.

MIRIAM

Oh really? Well, you might have been killed if I hadn't been watching you. You would have been killed in Pharaoh's court if I hadn't been there. Do you think it was an accident? "Can I get a nurse to suckle him for you highness?" I didn't have to do that.

AARON

God saw to it that you did.

MIRIAM

God saw to it. I wanted you to live. *I* did. And our mother and father did. How can you really believe that if God hadn't "seen to it" that we would have let you die?

AARON

Miriam, stop. We're together now. Can't we be a family? Just look at him – can't you see how he's changed?

MIRIAM

Well look at any of us, Aaron. We aren't children any more. All of us have changed.

AARON

But Moses has changed more than any of us.

MEN

Moses has seen the face of God!

AARON

He is more than he ever was – he –

MIRIAM

You all can worship him and stand against me if you want to. But just remember, Moses, I know you as you are.

MOSES

You see me as I was. The rest is history now, woman.

MIRIAM

Everything you are is because of woman. The woman who gave you life. The woman who took you in. The woman who came to you in the desert and married you. And this woman who watched you through it all.

AARON

It was Moses who went up to Sinai. Moses who stood in the presence of God.

MIRIAM

Maybe I've been in the presence of the SHEKHINAH too.

MEN

No!

WOMEN

Yes!

MOSES

Miriam. Be careful of what you say.

AARON

Blasphemer!

MEN

Blasphemer!

MIRIAM

Yes! Yes! That's what you call anyone who says something you don't choose to believe. But go ahead. Call your flesh and blood names if it makes you feel better. I know what I know.

WOMEN	MEN
Miriam knows!	Impossible Lies!

AARON

You see what happens? It's all because we let the people get so out of control!

WOMEN	MEN
Wild!	Drunk on our own fear and freedom. Insane!

MIRIAM

No. We gained control. When the people grew frightened and unnerved because you abandoned us – I know, I know – it was a holy quest. But Moses, you showed no signs of returning... could you blame them? If you'd never "seen the face" of God, would you have been patient?

39

MEN

He would have. Moses. Of course you would have!

MOSES

Yes! I stood with Him when He vowed to destroy you all. And I won forgiveness – for your sin!

MEN

Whose sin?

ALL

My sin?

WOMEN

Our sin?

MIRIAM

Yes, Moses, whose sin do you mean? The people – everyone was desperate for something real to connect them to the miracle that brought us across the sea.

WOMEN

Desperate!

MIRIAM

You had disappeared. They would have rioted if it hadn't been for us. So Aaron made a gold calf. So what? It kept them centered on something. We kept them here.

AARON

No, Miriam, he's right. We never should have made the calf.

MIRIAM

What other choice did the people give us Aaron? Tell me.

   (Silence)

(quietly) I can't stay.

MOSES

You can't leave.

MIRIAM

Is that for you to say? Everything your way? I'm listening, Moses. These are your people. I don't know if they're mine.

AARON

Miriam! Think about what you're saying!

MIRIAM

Aaron, don't you see how blind you've become? How you follow him without so much as a single question? None of you asks questions anymore!

AARON

God's word is not for you to question.

MIRIAM

Of course it is. And if I cannot question it here with you, I will question it alone with the SHEKHINAH.

MOSES

Imagine the chaos if everyone went wandering off into the desert, questioning God.

AARON

Here, in the wild, we need order. Not questions.

MIRIAM

(shouting) No! You're wrong!! You need questions!! I have questions! Can't you see how important that is?

MOSES

You're abandoning your people.

MIRIAM

If they think I've abandoned them then they're your people, not mine. As if people belong to anyone!

(Miriam turns away from the table)

MEN

Where is she going? Moses, where is Miriam going?

MOSES

She is cast into the desert alone.

ALL

What?

AARON

Because of her wickedness, leading you all in wild abandon, God is punishing her, making her a Leper.

(Pause. Everyone is shocked silent)

ZIPPORAH

What?

AARON

It is God's punishment for her wickedness in leading you all in drunken abandon – when you should have been praying for our safe deliverance!

ZIPPORAH

Really, Aaron. You led us too. You made the golden calf.

AARON

Come. Let us mourn the loss of our sister. And let us prepare to continue on our journey.

ZIPPORAH

(Pause. Then to Moses alone) Moses, the people listen to you. We all follow you. But Miriam is no more a leper than I am.

AARON

She's removed herself from us. Ostracized. What difference is there?

ZIPPORAH

Aaron, please. Give us just a moment. What difference is there, Moses? None to everyone else. But to me, the difference is as great as any one of the miracles we've seen. Don't look at me like that. We'll all do exactly as you say, no matter what that is. It's a lot of power you have, no matter where it comes from.

MOSES

You doubt the word of God?

ZIPPORAH

Moses, I believe that God has made you a great hero. But you are only a great leader because of the people around you. We make up for the simple acts that might waste your time.

MOSES

You disapprove of the way I've taken care of you? Of your father?

ZIPPORAH

Oh no. I know my place. But Miriam doesn't. And I'm glad for it. If you had it in you, you'd be glad too.

MOSES

I am grateful for my sister. But the people need justice and examples. Without that, they will run wild and there is no future for us. How will the people behave if their actions have no consequences?

ZIPPORAH

One thing has nothing to do with the other. I never said justice wasn't important. But compassion—

MOSES

God has compassion. He would have destroyed us all if he didn't.

ZIPPORAH

And you? What would you do?

MOSES

Miriam could never lead the people as I do. The weight of the decisions would crush her.

WOMEN	MEN
She understands us. Miriam knows the heart of her people	Miriam lead? We could never follow her anger.

ZIPPORAH

Miriam is angry, yes. But who here hasn't been? Moses, your mind shines brighter than the rest of us. You know ... so many things. But will you hold yourself so far above even those of us who love you the most? Your mind may shine brighter, but my father always told me that every person has something unique that only they can teach. You will never learn it if you don't listen.

WOMEN

Yes! Listen, Moses! Listen!

ZIPPORAH

(Picks up horseradish)

All of you! Look at this. All this bitterness – it's affecting us all. We're fighting among ourselves. It isn't any good. Not any of it.

הבה נזכור את נשמת כל חי, שמשמרת את זיכרון מרירותינו

HAVAH NIZKOR ET NISHMAT KOL CHAI, SHEVRISHAMERET ET ZICHERON MIRIRUTAYNU.

Come let us remember the soul of every living thing that remembers our bitterness. Yes, eat of your own bitterness. See what happens. See how it doesn't get sweet by itself.

(Everyone eats the horseradish)

Let your brilliant mind think on that for a while, Moses. Everyone. Just think about it.

MOSES

Zipporah. Wait. You don't understand.

ZIPPORAH

Of course not. I'm a mere woman. How could I possibly understand? Maybe Aaron can explain it to me. That's what he does. Explains things. What did Miriam do that was so terrible that she had to be cast out? Was she so wicked to challenge you both?

AARON

Miriam ostracized herself When someone shuts herself off from the rest of us, that is the wicked act.

ZIPPORAH

(to Moses and Aaron together) And when someone turns *his* back on *his* own flesh and blood?

MOSES

Must you think the worst of me?

43

ZIPPORAH

What else am I to think? When I see you treat your sister – you made everyone believe she was sinful. Did you make *her* believe you thought she was sinful?

MOSES

I would not think my sister wicked. But I would no more see her held captive by her own anger.

ZIPPORAH

You brought it on yourself.

MOSES

You would call me cruel for giving her the very thing she demanded and sorely needed. When Miriam returns, believe me, it will be to the sound of *all* of our voices singing for joy to see her again.

ZIPPORAH

(pause) Human after all, are you? Well, remember that, Moses.

(To all)

Miriam will return.

AARON

If she atones for —.

ZIPPORAH

And *when* she does, we all will welcome her back with song and timbrels. I'm not going anywhere until Miriam comes back, Moses. (To all) And neither are the rest of us!

WOMEN	MEN
We will wait for Miriam!	Moses – how will she return?

AARON

So we will wait for Miriam, then we will continue on to the promised land.

MOSES

All right, then. But we are still so far away. We can't wait for long.

ZIPPORAH

It is not so far. And we will wait.

Mortar
Russia, 1917

MARUSA

We heard the crash in the kitchen. At first, we thought it was my mother dropping the wine. With bitterness in our mouths, we stood shocked. Water and wine were splashed everywhere amid broken glass. The hooves that my father heard were real.

ELENA

How could this happen?

ALEXI

We didn't do anything.

MISHA

We were having a Passover Seder. That's doing something.

ELENA

Look at all of this. Shattered. Wine everywhere.

MISHA

These linens are ruined. And the glasses. Elena. I told you not to use the good crystal. Look at it now, absolutely destr —

ELENA

Alexi. Keep your hands away. That broken glass is sharp as a razor. Oh Misha, these were the glasses from our wedding.

ALEXI

I wasn't touching anything.

ELENA

Marusa. Stop daydreaming again. Come, help me clean some of this mess up. (To herself) I hardly know where to begin... Marusa! Come on.

MARUSA

(shaky, tearful) I'm sorry, Mama. Oh, Mama, Papa, Zaide. I'm so sorry!

MAYER

What is she talking about?

ELENA

Marusa. What are you sorry for?

MARUSA

It's all my fault. I just know it is.

MISHA

What do you mean, it's all your fault. Did you invite the Tsar's men for dinner?

MARUSA

No. But this afternoon... when I was playing in the kitchen and you were trying to set the table... you wanted me to help... and I wanted to play...

ELENA

Yes, so?

MARUSA

So I wished for something. I wished for something awful!

ALEXI

She's crazy. Marusa! You're crazy!

MARUSA

Oh no! I —

MAYER

What did you wish for, darling?

MARUSA

I wished... I wished that all the glasses were gone... so we wouldn't have to wash them all to set the table... Oh, Mama! I'm so sorry!!

MISHA

(reaches to touch Marusa's hand) Marusa. You didn't make the soldiers come tonight.

MARUSA

Oh, but Papa, I did. I wished for the glass to be gone. And now it's broken. It's all my fault.

MISHA

No. It isn't.

MARUSA

Then why? Why did they come?

MAYER

Oy. Why did they come? How could this happen? It happens because it's always happened. What I don't understand is how it can always happen to us.

(Alexi starts picking through the Charoset with a spoon)

46

ELENA

Would you listen to yourselves? Oy, this is horrible. Oy, this is disaster. Oy, oy, oy. It's Passover. It's a celebration of how disaster will not destroy us. We are not slaves here. We're not in the desert. Okay, so our lives aren't perfect either. But look around the table. We're together. A little glass? A little spilled wine? What's more important?

MISHA

Of course, Elena. You're right. You're right.

MAYER

Alexi. What are you doing?

ALEXI

There isn't any glass.

ELENA

What?

ALEXI

The glass. It didn't shatter into the charoset. We can still eat it.

ELENA

Are you sure? (Looks through it) He's right. The only thing on the table absolutely untouched. How did that happen? (Pause) Well, everyone. Eat then.

(Everyone eats some Charoset)

MISHA

It's a sign, you know. That God would leave us something sweet. We clean up the glass. We rebuild. We move on.

ELISHA

I'm sorry.

MAX

Stop saying that! Elisha, what do you have to be sorry for?

ELISHA

Oh. Of course. You're right. I'm sorry.

MAX

It's Mila who should be sorry. But Mila has no idea.

MILA

You're right. I have no idea. I will never be able imagine any of it. So how guilty should I feel for not being there with you?

MAX

I don't know. You tell me.

MILA

(pause) I'll never know what made any of you the way – I mean, what happened. There. I wasn't there at the camps with you. I came later. Last year. After the liberation. When you were in Poland, Aunt Elisha.

Poland, 1946

(Everyone except for Mila and Elisha holds hands so that Mila and Elisha are encircled by the rest of the group. The people sitting next to Mila and Elisha may need to stand behind them to achieve this effect. Mila takes a deep breath before speaking. She is exhausted and excited)

MILA

(to Elisha) Um, Hello?

(Elisha does not respond)

Excuse me?

ELISHA

Yes.

MILA

Um, I don't mean to bother you. But is your name Elisha?

ELISHA

(suddenly nervous) She's gone. I don't know where. Why? Who are you? Who wants to know?

MILA

I'm... It's not important. I thought you were... someone I knew.

ELISHA

I see.

MILA

I've come all the way from America, through Europe. Germany. I've been everywhere. You're – I mean, she's the last one I have any hope of finding.

ELISHA

Why? And what will you do when you find her?

MILA

Oh, well, take her back with me.

ELISHA

Back? Where? I'm not going back to Germany. Not back to the Nazis.

MILA

No. No, of course not. Never back there. I promise.

ELISHA

Not that anyone in Germany would remember me now.

MILA

Maybe not. But somewhere else, I'm sure there are people who remember you.

ELISHA

Remember me? Oh, I... I look quite different than I did back then. I'm sure no one would know me.

MILA

Oh. Well, you see, you look like someone... this picture.

ELISHA

Oh... where did you get this?

MILA

Aunt Elisha. Please. It's me. Mila.

ELISHA

No, Mila isn't here. She disappeared with her father... my brother... before all the trouble got bad.

MILA

No, Aunt Elisha. I am Mila. Please. Look at me.

(Elisha looks up)

I've come to take you home with me. Home. To America.

ELISHA

Mila? America?? How did – I don't understand.

MILA

Aunt Elisha. I've been searching all over Europe. For everyone. Please. Come home to us.

ELISHA

Mila...? Oh my...

(They embrace)

I can't imagine how it must be for you to see me this way. In a place like this. But there was no other place to go.

MILA

How did you —

ELISHA

It's a simple life, really. People mostly leave me alone. I think I scare some of them. But they don't ask me any questions. I don't bother anybody.

MILA

Aunt Elisha... I've been searching... everywhere... for two years.

ELISHA

(looking at the photograph) Look at that... Oh, but haven't you changed. My God, you were just a little girl then. (Looks up at Mila) and you found everyone?

MILA

Uncle Max... he's been waiting for you so anxiously. I found him first. Oh, he misses you so. Then Lisi and Asher. They got to see Papa, at least for a little while. Mama... I found her... her records. They were in Auschwitz.

ELISHA

What about Anna and Maike?

MILA

Aunt Elisha. I didn't know if I could find *anyone*. Everyone was so scattered. Nobody knew I was looking. It was like catching dust and feathers.

ELISHA

Oh, my dear. I didn't think I'd ever see anyone again.
        (She looks around)

ELISHA

Where is everyone?

MILA

(patiently) Waiting for you at home. In America. They're all celebrating Passover tonight. I can't wait to wire them that I found you.

ELISHA

Passover? Oh, do you remember how we celebrated Passover in the camps. Whispering in the darkness. Holding up a scrap of moldy bread as our matzah. Ha. Bread of affliction. Remember?

MILA

I wasn't there, Aunt Elisha.

ELISHA

No, no you're right. I'm sorry. Of course you weren't.

MILA

Come on. Let's pack your things.

ELISHA

I have everything I need. But we don't have anything for the Seder. You did say it was Passover? I didn't even remember. I... I don't talk to many people here.

MILA

It's okay, Aunt Elisha. We can —

(Elisha starts scrambling across the tablecloth, putting things together on her plate)

ELISHA

Oh dear. Nothing.

MILA

Well, maybe not. Some bread. A little mustard. An apple.

(Everyone makes a sandwich with maror, charoset and matzah.)

Aunt Elisha. Look. We'll make a little Hillel sandwich. See? This will be our matzah. And here's our bitter herbs. And a little slice of apple. Charoset. There. It's perfect.

(Everyone eats the sandwich)

ALL

This year we celebrate here.

ELISHA

Next year in Jerusalem.

MILA

In America.

Oh yes. Of course. You're right.

L'CHI LACH

Music: Debbie Friedman
Lyrics: Debbie Friedman & Savina Teubal
Based on Genesis 12: 1-2

14

Roasted Egg, Maternal/Eternal Regenerative Power
America, 1947

MILA

I wish Papa could see this. All of us together.

ASHER

And Mama, too.

LISI

Oh, Mama would have loved this, wouldn't she? Everything at the Seder always meant something for her.

MILA

Everything had a purpose, everything had a reason.

MAX

Well, everything doesn't have a reason. Even if it should have a place. Look at the egg on the plate. It sits there, roasted, but we don't ever say a word about it.

ELISHA

(just realizing) I know why the egg is on the plate. I think —

MAX

Eggs are for funerals.[9]

ELISHA

The egg is in the Seder because —

LISI

Well maybe the egg is just something sacred, white and whole

MAX

Burnt and cracked.

MILA

It's roasted, Uncle Max. It's supposed to be like that

ELISHA

It's there as a —

LISI

Mama used to say that the egg was lucky.[10]

ELISHA

It's —

---

[9]Chaim Raphael, *A Feast of History* (New York: Simon and Schuster, 1972), 14.
[10]Fredman, 138.

MILA

Oh, yes, remember, she would say that whoever had the egg after the two Seders would have a wish come true in the next year.

ELISHA

Maybe it's true.

MAX

You don't really believe that Elisha.

ELISHA

Of course, you're right. I– No. I *do* believe it. I do know about the egg. It's a story. Very old. I heard it as a child. Isn't that funny? I just remembered it now. Once, many years ago, in a little village near the country, there lived a man and a woman. They had the most successful chicken farm for miles around. That's how it began.

MILA

And?

ELISHA

And ... let me see. And... And... And everyone wondered how it could possibly be. Disease would blight all the other chicken farms. But the woman would sit up all night with her chickens and they would be healthy. Foxes would attack the other chicken farms. That's right. I remember. But the foxes wouldn't dare go near the chickens of this woman and this man. Until one night, a particularly clever and vicious fox broke into the chicken coops and killed every last one, leaving nothing alive and unbroken but a single egg.

The man and the woman awoke to the destruction.

ELISHA and MAX

"How could this happen to us?!"

ELISHA

they cried out. All they heard was silence. The woman raged against it because it angered her. Yet no matter how she yelled and screamed, the silence was stronger. Finally, desperately, she threw herself into the silence and disappeared.

MAX

The man decided that the silence could only mean one thing: God was severe. There was no reason for anything. Life was hard. Lonely and deserted, the man tried to rebuild the farm, but to no avail. He stared at the egg, demanding that it hatch. Nothing happened. Man and farm grew desolate together.

ELISHA

Now lost in silence, the woman found that she had developed a special kind of hearing. She could hear the past in the present. She could hear the future in the past. At first the cacophony had her confused. She tried to make sense of it but found herself distracted by a scratching sound. She did everything she could to shut it out so she could concentrate. She closed windows. Still the scratching. She shut doors. To no avail.

ELISHA

She squeezed her eyes shut, held herself very still and focused as deeply as she could on the chaos. It was only then that she could make out the sound of a consistent voice, coming through past present and future.

ASHER

"Mama,"

ELISHA

...she heard softly. She opened her eyes, looked around, only to hear the scratching sound again. She quickly shut it out and listened again.

LISI

"Mama,"

ELISHA

...she heard, and then,

MILA

"Mama,"

ELISHA

...yet again. Again she opened her eyes and realized that both the voice and the scratching were coming from the little egg. Without even thinking, she broke the silence, (To Lisi, Asher and Mila) "I'm here," she said, (to Max) "I'm here." And with that, she reappeared out of the silence.

(Elisha reaches for Max's hand and puts an arm around the person next to her.)

ELISHA

Her husband was so overwhelmed with joy that he began to weep, washing away the desolation. He buried his head in his wife's hair and kissed her.

(As Elisha continues to speak, everyone reaches out a hand or puts an arm around the person next to him/her)

ELISHA

Then the woman picked up the egg, held it in her hands and in that moment, the egg cracked open to reveal an impossible ten baby chicks.

(Elisha picks up her cup of wine)

The woman lifted them up, held them and each grew healthy and strong.

(Elisha puts the cup down, then looks around the table, warmed and satisfied at her story and at the connection she has brought about)

ELISHA

There we are, children. Sometimes, you have to listen. And sometimes you have to know what you're hearing. So.

THE MEAL IS SERVED.

Searching and Finding
Every time and place

MIRIAM

Let us begin the search. For what we need. For what we have lost.

(Everyone starts looking for the Afikoman. Whoever finds the Afikoman must wrap it in a napkin, then pass it from person to person. Zack, Marusa, Rosa and Asher stand in front of the Biblical characters with the bundled afikomen.[11])

MIRIAM

From where have you come?

ZACK

From Egypt.

ROSA

From Ignorance

MARUSA

From Fear.

ASHER

From Slavery.

MIRIAM

And where are you going?

ZACK

To Jerusalem.

ROSA

To Knowing

MARUSA

To Trust

ASHER

To Freedom.

MIRIAM

What have you brought to help you on your journey?

ZACK

This bread.

---

[11] A Mediterranean Seder tradition involves wrapping the afikoman in a napkin. Each participant then takes a turn carrying it. This is based on the words, "The children of Israel took their dough before it was leavened, with kneading troughs bound up in their clothes upon their shoulders," from Exodus 12:34. The leader then asks the youngest child who receives the pack last, "From where have you come?" the answer being, "From Egypt." Then the child is asked, "Where are you going?" then answers, "To Jerusalem." Finally, the leader asks what provisions the child has brought for the trip and the child indicates the afikomen in the pack. Fredman, 124.

MARUSA

These memories.

ROSA

This courage.

ASHER

This history.

MARUSA, ROSA, ZACK and ASHER

This family. These stories. This Afikoman.

(The napkin containing the Afikomen is opened and the Afikomen is shared with everyone to eat. Everyone returns to their seats and a third cup of wine is poured for all.

Grace, The Third Cup of Wine and Water in the Desert: Hope

MIRIAM

And so, with our history, our courage, our memories and bread within us, let us offer blessings of thanks.

לעולם נאחז בזכרונותנו ונביט לעתיד בתקוה.

L'OLAM N'ECHAZ B'ZICHRONOTEINU V'NABIT L'ATID BATIKVAH.

May we always hold tight to our past, even as we look ahead in hope for the future.

Birkat Hamazon

Music and lyrical adaptation by Corey-Jan Albert
Copyright 2009, Corey-Jan Albert, all rights reserved

(Everyone raises a glass of wine)

MIGUEL

נהליל את מקור החיים בורא פרי הגפן

N'HALEYL ET MEKOR HACHAYIM, BOREH P'RI HAGOFEN. Let us praise the source of life that brings forth fruit of the vine. Let us drink to the hope that helps us find our way home.

(Everyone drinks)

MARUSA

Out of our past.

MILA

Out of our fears.

(Everyone raises a glass of water)

MIRIAM

נהליל את המים מקור החיים.

N'HALEYL ET BOREH HA-MAYIM, MEKOR HACHAYIM. Let us celebrate the source of life that brings forth the well that sustains us in the desert.

(Everyone drinks.)

ELLIOT

So now we invite Elijah to join us at the table.

(Elliot takes Elijah's cup and passes it around the table. Everyone pours some wine from their cups to fill it.)

Each of us pours some wine into his cup, all of us acting together to make the world perfect for the messianic era. Michelle and Zack, go open the door. Now the door is open for —

ZACK

(while walking over to the door) Wouldn't it be cool if we opened the door and some old guy was there? He was a traveler or something? And he just walked right in and sat down at Elijah's place?

MICHELLE

Or a woman. I've read about stories where people during the Holocaust saw an old woman who gave them her last piece of bread and then later, there was no record of her – as if she didn't even ever exist.

ALISE

You know, actually, back in the middle ages, there were rumors that the Jews were actually doing ritual sacrifices, mixing Christian blood into the matzahs. That's probably one of the reasons why people opened the door during the Seder – to to show the outside world that this was a normal family celebration.[12]

ZACK

(disgusted and in disbelief) Are you serious?

ALISE

Oh yeah.

ELLIOT

Thankfully, we don't have to worry about that anymore. Just open the door, Zack.

(Zack opens the door)

Very good. Now the door is open for the possibility of a world united in trust and friendship. Okay, close the door now.

MICHELLE

Why don't we just leave it open for a while?

ELLIOT

Because it's night time, Michelle. And we don't live in a world of trust and friendship yet.

MICHELLE

I thought that was the point.

---

[12]Einstein, Stephen J. and Lydia Kukoff, *Every Person's Guide to Judaism* (New York: UAHC Press, 1989) 52.

ALISE

Opening the door is a symbolic gesture.

MICHELLE

Yeah, right. Another empty symbol.

MARUSA

(Sigh) Michelle, you're very young. You trust everybody. But you don't remember things. You don't remember how it happened. You don't remember how it begins!!

MICHELLE

Grandma, what are you talking about?

MARUSA

I'm talking about how it happened. How it always happens! Like this – look – you've got the door wide open!! Why would you leave the door wide open like that?!

ZACK

Um, for Elijah?

MARUSA

Elijah. You think Elijah is some magic man who's going to come waltzing through that door? Let me tell you – With the doors wide open, soldiers will come sweeping through, smashing everything.

MICHELLE

Grandma, there aren't any soldiers.

MARUSA

That's what you think. You think that the stories you hear are just stories - make believe. That's what I once thought. You think those kinds of things when you're young. You trust everyone. But let me tell you, you can't always trust people.

MICHELLE

Maybe that's the trouble. Maybe the trouble is when you don't trust people, Grandma.

ALISE

Michelle!

MARUSA

Maybe the trouble is when you don't just let well enough alone. All night long, you wouldn't let us get on with the Seder. All night, you've got things to say.

MICHELLE

All night long– you think that I– Then forget it. Just forget it. Forget I ever said anything.
        (She gets up, goes to the door and goes outside, slamming it behind her. Alise and Marusa get up to go after her. Everyone else follows.)

More Questions
Outside/The Desert, Indeterminate Time

MICHELLE

Forget I ask questions. I mean, it's not like I'm supposed to ask them, right? Why is this night different from any other night? A big dinner, that's all. I know some awful things have happened to our family in the past. But what am I supposed to do with that? Why do bad things keep happening to the Jews anyway? If it's going to keep happening, why bother?

MICHELLE and MIRIAM

Why bother with any of it?

MIRIAM

Moses goes off alone and the people fall apart. He goes up to find God and returns victorious, as if he's been back from war. War. War. Well, we're not in Egypt anymore, Moses. We're out in the desert. Who will you fight now? If you can't fight Pharaoh, who will you turn on so that you can be righteous?

MIRIAM	MIGUEL
What would he have me do?	What would she have me do?

MIGUEL

Leave our home? Leave all that we've worked so hard to build? I'm not the idiot she must think me to be. I know they have no love for us. So I am saving our lives.

MIGUEL and MILA

You don't understand any of this, do you?

MILA

You argue and fight over what was real. And over what's real now.

ASHER

Mila, he only wants to remember the bad parts.

MAX

And he only wants to forget.

MILA, MIGUEL and MIRIAM

Must it always be an argument? Do we always have to find adversaries among ourselves?

MAX

The adversaries are everywhere. If you'd been with us there, you would know, Mila. But I can tell you that the adversaries don't go away just because you forget. What will happen fifty or sixty years from now when there's nobody left to remember?

MIGUEL

Sooner or later, they will forget all about us. The dust will settle. And our children will be here. Alive and living in the houses of our determination.

ARTURO and ASHER

Then it will be over.

MAX

No. Then it will begin again.

MILA

I searched the whole world just to bring our family back together. But it didn't work the way I'd planned. Even arguing, you know something that I never will.

MILA and MIRIAM

I wasn't there with you. And so I'm apart.

MIRIAM

But I heard the voice of God as clearly as you did. I didn't look up to find the Ruler of the Universe to lead us away. I listened for something softer, glorious, that dwells in our midst. When I heard, it sounded like music. And I was not afraid to sing.

MIGUEL and MIRIAM

But I'm utterly alone, do you hear?

ARTURO

No you're not. I'm right here with you. See?

MIGUEL

Yes. Yes, of course, you are.

MIGUEL, ELISHA and MIRIAM

But still, I feel lost.

ARTURO

Lost?

MIGUEL

Yes, maybe that's just what we are.

ARTURO

How can we be lost? We walked here. We can walk back home.

MIGUEL and MIRIAM

If only it were really so simple. To just turn around and go home. How can I go back after leaving the way I did?

ARTURO

It is that simple. See? We step. Then we step again. And we walk. And we go down that path and over the bridge. And then we are home.

ALISE

Michelle, please come back inside.

MARUSA

Your old grandmother just got carried away.

MICHELLE

Just forget it.

MARUSA

No, we won't. Because that's what you do with memories. You remember them. They're part of who we are. Not just our own stories. Not even just my stories. But *all* the stories, all the memories. That's why we tell them. That's why they're more than just stories. They're part of you, just like they are part of me and all the people who lived them and told them before.

MAX

You can't forget about things, even if you want to. Even if you weren't there. You've got to remember them, full and loud and smelly. You've got to make the memories real.

ELISHA

And if you can't hear your own memories, listen to their echoes. Listen.

MARUSA

It's when you shove the memories down that you get nightmares.

MIRIAM

When I went forth from Egypt.

MARUSA

Listen.

ALL

When we went forth from Egypt.

ARTURO

Do you think my parents are having a Seder somewhere, Tio Miguel?

MIGUEL

I hope so, Arturo.

MARUSA

Maybe there are millions of Seders happening tonight.

MIRIAM

We opened our hearts to the pain of our enslavement. To know the possibility of home.

MICHELLE

And maybe with all the doors open, it's all connected.

MIRIAM

The memories and the pain and hope and the possibility.

65

ALL

We live to tell the tale.

ARTURO

Tio Miguel?

MARUSA

And maybe that's where we get the strength to go on.

MARUSA

So, Michelle? What do you say - are we going to go back in? Because if we're going to stay out here all night, I'm going to need a blanket.

ARTURO

Can we go back now?

MIRIAM, MIGUEL and MILA

We cannot turn around to go backwards. We can only turn around to go forwards.

MICHELLE

Come on.

(Everyone walks back into the house together, holding hands, arms extended to one another, embracing.)

MICHELLE

We sat here, in our dining room, with more food than we could eat, more wine than we could drink, retelling the story of those with no time for bread to rise. And of those who had no bread at all.

AARON

What purpose could there have been in Pharaoh's harsh decrees?

MILA

What justice in death?

MARUSA

What reason in massacres?

MAX

No reason. No purpose. No justice. No sense.

ROSA

The artist creates from chaos.

MAYER

The reader knows what makes people the way they are.

ALEXI

The scientist knows that every individual is essential to the whole.

LISI

The mathematician knows that chaos holds precision.

MARUSA

The historian knows events spiral, echoing the past with every revolution.

ELISHA

The parent knows heartbreak and hope.

MAX

We eat the bread of affliction every year. We taste bitter herbs.

LISI

We mix them with the sweetness of hope for redemption.

ABUELA

Telling our history, asking these questions, every year, echoing the past with every revolution.

MIRIAM, MOSES, AARON, ZIPPORAH, SHIRA

"Once we were slaves in Egypt.

ALL

Next year may all be free."

ELENA

Look around the table. Look around our world. One of us knows things that others do not.

MIRIAM

One of us recognizes the truth.

MAURA

One of us knows human nature

ALISE

One of us can see how it fits together

MOSES

One of us can envision the plan

MIGUEL

One of us can inspire others to act.

ZACK

Each of us knows a question.

ALL

Each of us knows an answer.

ZIPPORAH

When we all act on what we know, when we accept each other as one family, we will finally shake off the bonds of slavery.

MICHELLE

Because none of us is free until all of us are free.

ALISE

In the glow of candles and the love of friends and family

ASHER

We must be true to ourselves.

(Everyone raises a glass of wine)

ROSA

To what we see.

MARUSA

To what we know.

MICHELLE

And to what we can do.

MAURA

נהליל את מקור החיים בורא פרי הגפן

N'HALEYL ET MEKOR HACHAYIM, BOREH P'RI HAGOFEN.
Let us praise the source of life that brings forth fruit of the vine.

(Everyone drinks)

MISHA

The stories of our history have been etched into our souls.

SHIRA

Like ancient music. You remember.

ELISHA and MARUSA

We can hear it.

ALL

And we will not be afraid to sing.

MILA

This year, we rejoice together.

ALL

Next year, may all rejoice in freedom.

לשנה הבאה בירושלים.
L'SHANAH HABA-AH, B'RUSHALAYIM
NEXT YEAR IN JERUSALEM!

Singing

Suggested songs:
B'shanah Haba-ah
Hineh Ma Tov
Miriam's Song
Chad Gad Yah
Let My People Go

Select Bibliography

Antonelli, Judith S. *In The Image of God: A Feminist Commentary on the Torah.* New Jersey: Jason Aronson, Inc., 1995.

Armstrong, Karen. *A History of God: The 4000-Year Quest of Judaism, Christianity and Islam.* New York: Alfred A. Knopf, 1993.

Broner, E.M. *The Telling.* San Francisco: HarperCollins, 1993.

Bronstein, Herbert, ed. *A Passover Haggadah.* New York: Central Conference of American Rabbis, 1982.

Deluxe Edition Passover Haggadah. Glenville, Illinois: Kraft General Foods, Inc., 1996.

Einstein, Stephen J. and Lydia Kukoff, *Every Person's Guide to Judaism.* New York: UAHC Press, 1989.

Elstein, Rochelle Berger, ed. *Why Is This Night Different.* Chicago: Northwestern University Press, 1990.

Falk, Marcia. *The Book of Blessings.* New York: HarperCollins, 1996.

Fredman, Ruth Gruber. *The Passover Seder.* Philadelphia: University of Pennsylvania Press, 1981.

Glatzer, Nahum N., ed. *The Passover Haggadah.* New York: Schocken Books, 1953.

Glick, Stephanie. *A Short History of the Passover Seder.* Paper presented at Congregation Beth Elohim, Acton, Massachusetts, April 1992, The Student & Academics Department Archives of The World Zionist Organization.

Kaplan, Mordecai M., Eugene Kohn and Ira Eisenstein for the Jewish Reconstructionist Foundation, ed. *The New Haggadah for the Pesah Seder.* New York: Behrman House, 1941.

Levy, Shimon. "The Passover Haggadah as a Tangible Act of Performance." trans. Bonnie and Joel Goobich. In *The Altar and The Stage.* Tel Aviv, Israel: Or-am, 1992.

Plaskow, Judith. *Standing Again at Sinai.* San Francisco: Harper, 1990.

Raphael, Chaim. *A Feast of History: Passover Through The Ages as a Key to Jewish Experience.* New York: Simon and Schuster, 1972.

Schechner, Richard. *Essays on Performance Theory, 1970 - 1976.* New York: Drama Book Specialists, 1977.

Sholem, Gershom G. *Major Trends in Jewish Mysticism.* New York: Schocken Books, 1961.

Strassfeld, Michael, ed. "A Passover Haggadah," in *Conservative Judaism.* New York: The Jewish Theological Seminary of America, 1979.

The Torah: The Five Books of Moses. Philadelphia: The Jewish Publication Society of America, 1962.

Turner, Victor. *The Drums of Affliction*. London: Oxford University Press, 1968.

Turner, Victor. "Introduction." In *Celebration: Studies in Festivity and Ritual*, ed. Victor Turner. Washington, DC: Smithsonian Institution Press, 1982.

Turner, Victor. *From Ritual to Theatre*. New York: Performing Arts Journal Publications, 1982.

Van Gennep, Arnold. *The Rites of Passage*. trans. Monika B. Vizedom and Gabrielle L. Caffee. Chicago: The University of Chicago Press, 1960.

Waskow, Arthur. *The Shalom Seders*. New York: Adama Books, 1984.

Endnotes

[1]Chaim Raphael, *A Feast of History: Passover Through The Ages as a Key to Jewish Experience* (New York: Simon and Schuster, 1972) 11.

[2]Rochelle Berger Elstein, ed., *Why is This Night Different* (Chicago: Northwestern University Press, 1990) 1.

[3]Nahum N. Glatzer, ed., *The Passover Haggadah* (New York: Schocken Books, 1953), 11.

[4]*Ibid.,* 111.

[5]Arthur Waskow, *The Shalom Seders* (New York: Adama Books, 1984) 7.

[6]Numbers 12.

[7]Karen Armstrong, *A History of God: The 4000-Year Quest of Judaism, Christianity and Islam,* (New York: Alfred A. Knopf, 1993), 50.

[8]*Ibid.*, 52.

[9]Judith Plaskow, *Standing Again at Sinai*, (San Francisco: Harper, 1990) 38.

[10]Shimon Levy, "The Passover Haggadah as a Tangible Act of Performance,"in *The Altar and The Stage.* Israel: Or-am, 1992, typescript translated by Joel and Bonnie Goobich, 11.

[11]Raphael, 13.

[12]Fredman, 115.

[13]Glatzer, 29.

[14]Glatzer, 9-10.

[15]Fredman, 142.

[16]Raphael, 14.

[17]Fredman, 118.

[18]Numbers 20:1-2, Talmud Bavli, Ta'anit 9a, and Nachmanides; Ta. 9a; *Zohar* II:190b, as quoted in Judith S. Antonelli, *In The Image of God: A Feminist Commentary on the Torah* (New Jersey: Jason Aronson, Inc., 1995), 173.

[19]Fredman, 18.

[20]Marcia Falk, *The Book of Blessings* (New York: HarperCollins, 1996), xvii.

[21]E.M. Broner, *The Telling* (San Francisco: HarperCollins, 1993), 77.

[22]Gershom G. Sholem, *Major Trends in Jewish Mysticism* (New York: Schocken Books, 1961), 230.

[23]Falk, xviii.

[24]*Ibid.,* xvii.

[25]Peshahim 116a, as quoted in Glatzer, 22-23.

[26]Glatzer, 23.